Early N   ty

Mathematic
3 to 5

Early Numeracy

Mathematical Activities
for 3 to 5 year olds

MARGARET SANGSTER
AND RONA CATTERALL

continuum

Continuum International Publishing Group
The Tower Building   80 Maiden Lane, Suite 704
11 York Road   New York, NY 10038
London
SE1 7NX

www.continuumbooks.com

© Margaret Sangster and Rona Catterall 2009

British Library Cataloguing-in-Publication Data
A catalogue record for this book is available from the British Library.

ISBN: 9781847064998 (paperback)

Library of Congress Cataloging-in-Publication Data
Sangster, Margaret.
  Early numeracy : mathematical activities for 3 to 5 year olds / Margaret Sangster and Rona Catterall.
    p. cm.
  ISBN 978-1-84706-499-8 (pbk.)
  1. Mathematics—Study and teaching (Preschool)—Activity programs. 2. Education, Preschool—Activity programs. I. Title.
  QA135.6.S26 2009
  372.7—dc22
2009006006

Typeset by Ben Cracknell Studios | www.benstudios.co.uk
Printed and bound in Great Britain by CPI Antony Rowe, Chippenham, Wiltshire

Contents

Introduction

This book is about young children learning mathematics. To those of us who have been through school as pupils it is hard to remember how challenging it is to learn to count. Looking back, it is as if it happened instantly and for some children that might be true, for others it might have taken a considerable amount of time. As adults we are often not aware of the many aspects of mathematics that have to be understood before children are able to use the symbolic language of mathematics. For example, how quickly do children realize that numbers have to come in order, that the last number you say is the name of the quantity you are counting and you can start to count a group anywhere? The activities in this book are at a level for children beginning to experience mathematics either in the nursery, playschool or Reception class (3–5 years). It may also be of use to those who are working with slightly older children who find learning mathematics challenging.

This book contains many activities which can be used by adults to develop young children's mathematics. There are suggestions of ways the activities can be made to be different, or harder and sometimes easier. There is also a section which considers the mathematics involved and issues around each aspect of mathematics. We chose to arrange the activities under different resource headings – the kind of resources that can be found in most reception and nursery classes – but we recognize the importance of visiting the same mathematics using different contexts and resources. This enables children to realize what is common to different situations and what can be transferred to new situations. The Mathematics Links Grid shows the main mathematical content of each activity so that you can move to a different activity but with a similar mathematical emphasis. Sometimes it is hard to think of the kind of questions that will help children to learn, so we have included some questions which will help you to run the activity. No doubt, you will have others to ask as well.

How to use this book

We have used the word teacher in all the activities to represent the adult who is working with the group and is proactive in teaching the children. In some activities and situations the teacher takes on an instructional approach, in others the teacher acts as a facilitator to encourage children's thinking.

There are many ways to use the activities to suit your specific situation or needs. You may choose to use an activity with all the children to start a session (starter) or to finish a session (plenary). You may choose to run the activity with all the children and then allow one small group to repeat the activity with adult support. You may decide to set the activity up for a small group of children for whom you think this learning is appropriate, or you may set the activity up so that children can visit it as they please. Once the children are familiar with some of the activities, they may be able to visit them without adult support. Young children like to revisit their favourite activities many times. This gives them confidence and consolidates their learning. If children feel confident and enjoy the task, they will be motivated to engage further and learning is likely to take place.

We have included a grid which will allow you to see the activities at a glance but also it indicates the mathematics that it is possible to engage with when doing the activity. You may choose to use the resource and visit different aspects of mathematics or you may wish to choose a mathematical idea and visit it several times using different resources. Or you may wish to visit an activity lots of times because you and the children find it fun!

Finally, we very much hope that you find the book helps you to engage the children in learning early mathematics, but most of all we hope you and your children enjoy the activities as well as learn from them.

Mathematics link grid

	Page number	Sorting/matching	Number word order	Counting – objects	Counting dots, pictures and so on	Counting up-on/down/back	Counting in 2s/5s/10s	Number symbols – ordering	Number symbols – reading
Number rhymes									
Five brown teddy bears	14		•			•			
The big clock	16		•	•				•	•
The silly clowns	18		•			•			
Sweets for sale	20		•			•			
The balloons	22		•	•					
The Christmas trees	24		•	•					
Five busy bees	26		•			•			
The postman	28		•	•					
A pair of legs	30		•				•		
We like numbers	32								•
Dice									
If it's a 3 clap our hands	36			•	•				•
Dots on top	38	•			•				•
More or less	40				•				
Match the objects	42	•		•	•				
Adders	43				•				
Count on	44				•	•			
The hidden face	46				•				
Money, money, money	48				•				
More money	50				•	•			
Two snake race	51				•				
Mystery number	52				•				•
Jump to it	54				•				•
Floor activities									
The windmill track	58		•			•			•
The side-by-side track	60		•			•			•
The single track	62		•			•			•
The stepping stone track	64		•			•			•
Islands	66		•	•					•
Four corners	68								•
Find your seat	70		•	•					•
Catching the train	72		•	•					•
The noise-maker	74		•	•					•
Copy cats	76		•	•					
Number lines									
Pegging out	80		•					•	•
Before and after	82		•					•	•
Here's Hoppy	84		•					•	•
Missing numbers	86		•					•	•
Hop on and back	88		•			•	•	•	•
Pegging pairs	90		•				•	•	•

Number symbols – writing	Conversation	Equivalence/partitioning	Addition/combining sets	Subtracting/taking /difference	Ordinal numbers – oral	Money/coinage	Number bonds	Language of positioning/movement	Comparing measures, length and so on	Estimation	Probability	2D shape
				•				•				
				•								
				•		•						
				•								
				•								
				•								
	•											
								•				
•												
			•	•				•				
			•									
							•					
				•			•	•				
						•						
						•						
						•						
								•				
								•				

	Page number	Sorting/matching	Number word order	Counting – objects	Counting dots, pictures and so on	Counting up-on/down/back	Counting in 2s/5s/10s	Number symbols – ordering	Number symbols – reading
Finger counting									
Fish fingers	94		•	•					
Up-down fingers	96		•	•					
Bunches of fives	98		•	•					
Finger prints	100		•	•					
Five finger exercise	102		•				•		
Fist towers	104		•	•					
Dominoes									
Who has …?	108			•	•				
Let's play dominoes	110	•		•	•				
Line up	112			•	•				
2D shape									
Find me	116	•		•					
Tell me something about …	118			•					
It's different because …	120			•					
Shape snake	122			•					
Boxes, bottles and bags									
Hiding	126								•
Take five	128		•						
Posting boxes	130		•		•				•
Green bottles	132		•	•					
Number boxes	134		•	•					•
Shelling out	136			•					
Look and tell	138								
Wet, wet, wet	140								
Cubes									
Build a tower	144								
Number towers	146			•					•
Which is missing?	147			•					•
Passengers on the bus	148			•					
Cube collection	150			•	•				
Give and take	152			•	•				
What's next?	154			•	•				
Colour coding	156	•		•					
Softly, softly	158			•				•	
What's under the cloth?	160			•					
Other resources									
Long, longer, longest	164								
Stones	166								
Toys go home	168								•
Toys on the move	170								•
Bee Bop	172								
Join the dots	174								
Fishing for fives	176				•				•

Number symbols – writing	Conversation	Equivalence/partitioning	Addition/combining sets	Subtracting/taking /difference	Ordinal numbers – oral	Money/coinage	Number bonds	Language of positioning/movement	Comparing measures, length and so on	Estimation	Probability	2D shape
	•											
	•											
	•											
									•			
			•									
												•
												•
												•
												•
	•	•										
•					•			•	•			
•	•		•									
										•		
												•
	•								•			
									•			
			•	•								
											•	
			•	•								
									•			
									•			
								•				
									•			
•												

Number rhymes

Stories, songs and rhymes capture children's imagination. Young children particularly enjoy songs and rhymes that have repetition. As the words become familiar then they can join in. As far as mathematics is concerned, this is particularly useful, as the repetition helps to consolidate things such as reciting the number name order, counting backwards, and taking one away. We use rhymes to recall and apply knowledge all through life. For example, who has not used 'Thirty days hath September . . .'?

There are various nursery rhymes and songs to choose from which contain a mathematical aspect. It is important to tease out the mathematics so as to ensure that it matches a child's number ability. One needs to ask if it will confuse children who cannot say the number word order from one to ten correctly, if they learn a rhyme containing counting in 2s, or a song that counts down from ten to one? It may be that learning the rhyme will help the child remember and understand the maths. Interestingly, the most common number rhymes use counting down or taking away.

This section contains new number rhymes specially designed to contain a specific number aspect.

Before using any song or rhyme it is a useful strategy to check the mathematics it contains in order to match the mathematics to the children's needs and ability. It is surprising how many rhymes contain counting down.

Below is a short list of some well-known songs and rhymes, and the mathematics they contain:

Nursery rhyme	Mathematics
Ten fat sausages sizzling in a pan	Counting down in 2s from 10
One man went to mow	Starting at 1 and adding 1 Counting down
One, two, buckle my shoe	The number order: 1–2, 3–4, 5–6, 7–8, 9–10
Ten green bottles hanging on the wall	Starting at 10 and taking away 1
Five current buns in a baker's shop	Starting with 5 and taking away 1
This little pig went to market	One-to-one correspondence
There were ten in a bed	Starting at 10 and taking away 1
Let everyone clap hands like me	One-to-one correspondence Copying two actions
One, two, three, four five	The number order 1–5, 6–10

ACTIVITY 1
Five brown teddy bears

Purpose
Subtracting 1 and counting down.

Vocabulary
Numbers five to zero.

Resources
Five teddy bears and a box decorated to represent a wall, or pictures of five teddy bears (cut out) and a picture of a wall.

Activity

Based around the following rhyme (use the tune of 'Ten green bottles standing on a wall'):

> Five brown teddy bears sitting on the wall.
> Five brown teddy bears sitting on the wall.
> If one brown teddy bear should accidentally fall
> There'd be four brown teddy bears sitting on the wall.
>
> Four brown teddy bears sitting on the wall . . .
> [and so on, to:]
> . . . No brown teddy bears sitting on the wall.

Engage the children in discussion as you place each of the five teddy bears on the wall. For example, 'We have one brown teddy bear and another one. How many can we see on the wall?' 'Yes, we have two brown teddy bears on the wall. And here is another one. How many have we got now?' 'Let's count: one, two, three – three brown teddy bears sitting on the wall', and so on. Continue until all five teddy bears are sitting on the wall.

Sing the 'Five brown teddy bears' rhyme, above, to the children but stop and let them fill in the missing numbers. If necessary, count the bears to check the answer.

To begin, you can remove the 'fallen' teddy bear, then later a child can do so. Ensure that the 'fallen' bear is chosen randomly and is not always the next in the line.

When counting the bears on the wall, sometimes count right to left and sometimes left to right.

At the end of the song, to reinforce the counting down numbers say, 'five, four, three, two, one, no teddy bears, they're all gone'.

Use the fingers on one hand to illustrate and reinforce counting down (five, then four, then three, then two, then one, then none left).

With practice, the children will be able to sing the complete song. When they are familiar with the song and the counting down, ask the children to predict the answer. For example, 'There are four teddy bears on the wall, if one falls off how many will be left?'

Extension
- Slowly add to the line of teddy bears until there are ten.

Mathematical development
The counting of the teddy bears needs to be applied flexibly so that the children see you can count objects in any order.

ACTIVITY 2
The big clock

Purpose
Matching an amount to a spoken number and matching an amount to a written number on a clock face.

Vocabulary
Fast and slow, early and late, day and night, hours and minutes.

Resources
A large clock face.

Activity

Based around the following rhyme:

I have a big clock
All day long it goes Tic-Toc
But everyday at 1 o'clock
It goes BONG.

I have a big clock
All day long it goes Tic-Toc
But everyday at 2 o'clock
It goes BONG, BONG.

Teach the children 'The big clock' rhyme. Initially keep to the times of 1, 2 and 3 o'clock.

Add the actions:

I have a big 'clock' – draw a large circle in the air.

All day long it goes 'Tic-Toc' – use the index finger and move it from side to side like a metronome.

But everyday at 2 o'clock – hold up two fingers.

It goes BONG, BONG – these are said loudly and at the same time clap hands the correct number of times.

When the children know 'The big clock' rhyme and actions, add more times. With a number larger than three it is easy for the children to lose count, so you may need to count the number of BONGs. Do not always work consecutively; it makes it more fun and means the children have to listen more carefully if you move from say 4 o'clock to 1 o'clock and then to 5 o'clock.

Show the children a clock face. Put it to the time you are going to use in the next verse of the rhyme. After this has been done several times, stop saying the time and just point to the clock face so the children will have to read the 'o'clock' number, and then use the correct number of BONGs and claps.

Extension
- Some children may be able to use all the numbers from 1 to 12.
- Discuss with the children the different types of clocks and where they might see them. Make a collection of real clocks and watches and of pictures of timepieces.

Mathematical development
Telling the time is complicated as it involves two scales. A simple 'on the hour' introduction helps the children become familiar with the clock face.

ACTIVITY 3
The silly clowns

Purpose
Counting, matching written number symbols and spoken numbers.

Vocabulary
Numbers one to five.

Resources
A set of large cards numbered 0 to 5, and five cut-out pictures of clowns.

Activity

Based around the following rhyme:

One silly clown was juggling
High in the air on a narrow swing
He was having such great fun
He called another clown to come.

Two silly clowns were juggling
High in the air on a narrow swing
They were having such great fun
They called another clown to come
[– and so on, to:]

Five silly clowns were juggling
High in the air on a narrow swing
But all of a sudden the swing broke
And down fell these silly folk.
5, 4, 3, 2, 1, 0

Now no silly clowns are juggling
High in the air on a narrow swing
They're waiting for the repairman to come
So that they can have some fun.

Discuss with the children what clowns do, how they would recognize a clown, why clowns are funny, why do they act in a silly way. Say 'The silly clown' rhyme to the children. Illustrate it with clown cut-out pictures. Repeat the rhyme and encourage the children to join in.

After each verse, ask the children, 'How many clowns are there on the swing now?' Use the number cards so the children can see the numeral as they hear the spoken number.

Extension
- Taking the rhyme from one and going to ten may be too tedious. However, it is possible to begin the rhyme at a larger number, such as five clowns, and go up to ten.

Mathematical development
Ordering the numbers is an important part of learning the counting rhyme. Counting down or backwards will help the children later on to learn subtraction. Most children enjoy counting down.

ACTIVITY 4
Sweets for sale

Purpose
Counting down and exchanging money for an object.

Vocabulary
Pence, numbers one to five.

Resources
Five 1p coins (ideally real coins should be used) and five small sweets.

Activity

Based around the following rhyme where the children's names can be substituted:

Five sweets on a shelf by the door
Ann came and bought one
Then there were four.

Four sweets in a box for all to see
John came and bought one
Then there were three.

Three sweets, those you like to chew
Sahed came and bought one
Then there were two.

Two sweets were melting in the sun
Joe came and bought one
Then there was one.

One sweet all alone,
The others had gone
Rhea came and bought one
Then there were none.

Give each child a 1 pence coin, explain whose head is on the coin, show them where they can see the number 1 and read the writing to them 'one penny'. Show the children the five small sweets and explain that one of the 1-penny (1-pence) coins will buy one of the sweets.

Say 'The sweet shop' rhyme to the children, repeat it a few times.

Put the five sweets on a table and appoint a child as shopkeeper.

Then repeat the rhyme, but before each verse give one child in the class a 1-penny coin. Use the child's name, and as the child's name is spoken the child gives the shopkeeper the coin and chooses a sweet.

Repeat until all the sweets have been sold.

Extension
- Put up the price of the sweets to 2p each. Give the children either a 2p coin or two 1p coins.

Mathematical development
Fewer and fewer people use cash to pay bills, so many of the children may not have had experience of using coins. It may therefore be necessary to talk about buying from the shops. How do we pay for the things we buy? What kind of coins might be in a purse? N.B. Pence is plural, penny is singular, but common usage is pence for both.

ACTIVITY 5
The balloons

Purpose
Counting 1 to 5
and taking away 1.

Vocabulary
Numbers one to
five.

Resources
Five large circles painted different colours
with a string attached to each one. Arrange
them to represent a set of balloons (although
it is much more fun to have five real balloons
to pop).

Activity

Based around the following rhyme:

5 big balloons
Hanging in a tree
All at once
One went . . . POP.

4 big balloons
Hanging in a tree
All at once
One went . . . POP.

Continue to: 1 big balloon
Hanging in a tree
All at once
One went . . . POP.

The children count the balloons before each verse.

At the word POP a representational balloon is removed, or better still a real balloon is popped. (Popping real balloons can be exciting or scary.)

'How many balloons are there left?' The balloons are counted to check.

Continue until all the balloons are popped. When the rhyme is completed, ask questions such as 'How many balloons were there to begin with?' How many balloons were there at the end?' 'How many balloons were popped altogether?'

Use the fingers of one hand to illustrate counting down. First we had five balloons – five fingers, 'pop' – a finger goes down, and so on. Let the children show the counting down using their fingers.

Extension
• Have more balloons.

Mathematical development
Look for children who rely upon counting each time and do not have the understanding or confidence to know how many balloons will be left when one is popped.

ACTIVITY 6
The Christmas trees

Purpose
Counting 1 to 5, taking away 1, using the language of positioning.

Vocabulary
Numbers five to one.

Resources
Five Christmas trees painted, individually, on a piece of card. (Alternatively use five small artificial Christmas trees.)

Activity

Based around the following rhyme:

Five small Christmas trees standing on the floor
*_____ put one on the cupboard
And then there were four

Four small Christmas trees, I can see
*_____ put one on the table
And then there were three.

Three small Christmas trees in pots painted blue
*_____ put one on the bookshelf
And then there were two.

Two small Christmas trees shining in the sun
*_____ put one in the corner
And then there was one.

One small Christmas tree all alone
*_____ gave it to the teacher
And teacher took it home.

Say 'The Christmas tree' rhyme to the children replacing *_____ with the name of a child in the class. This child moves the Christmas tree to the new position.

The children count the Christmas trees before each verse.

The second lines can be changed to suit the classroom, for example put it under the clock, beside the sink, next to the goldfish bowl. This also means different positioning words can be used.

When the rhyme is completed, ask questions such as, 'How many Christmas trees were there to begin with?' 'Which Christmas tree did the teacher get?'

Show the children how to use the fingers of one hand to illustrate the counting down, 'First we had five Christmas trees' (five fingers are used), '*_____ moved one tree' (a finger goes down) 'so we had how many? Yes, we had four' . . . and so on.

Extension
A rhyme about Christmas is seasonal but it can easily be adapted to become a rhyme about, for example, five new pencils:
> Five new pencils in a box on the floor.
> Four new pencils straight for all to see.
> Three new pencils striped red and blue.
> Two new pencils lying in the sun.
> One new pencil, left all alone.

Mathematical development
Continue to familiarize the children with numbers so they are confident enough to see the patterns of five, four, three, two and one, and do not need to re-count. Contexts such as rhymes give opportunities to 'apply' maths.

ACTIVITY 7
Five busy bees

Purpose
Counting 1 to 5, using ordinal language – first, second, third, fourth, fifth.

Vocabulary
Numbers one to five, first, second, third, fourth and fifth.

Resources
A large picture of a beehive, five bees painted, individually, on a piece of card. (Alternatively dress five children to represent bees – use headbands with antennae, and black and yellow striped cloaks.)

Activity

Based around the following rhyme:

Five busy bees live in the beehive
One, two, three, four, five
They all go to find honey for tea
Some for you and some for me.

The first busy bee comes back
to the beehive
Buzz, buzz, buzz, says she
I've got some honey for your tea.

The second busy bee comes back
to the beehive
Buzz, buzz, buzz, says she
I've got some honey for your tea.

Continue with: The third busy bee . . . The fourth busy bee . . . The fifth busy bee . . .

> They've all come back with honey for tea
> Some for you and some for me
> Five busy bees back home in the beehive
> One, two, three, four, five.

Five children are selected to represent the bees. They stand in a line near the beehive. Ask the children 'How many bees are there?' Count, then say, 'We have five bees. This is the first bee, this is the second bee . . . this is the fifth bee.'

Say the rhyme and during the line, 'They all go to find honey for tea', the five bees move to different parts of the room.

At the line, 'The first busy bee comes back to the beehive', the first child returns (buzzes) and sits by the hive. Continue with the second, third, fourth and fifth bee. During the last verse the bees are re-counted.

Extension
- During the rhyme, various questions can be asked, such as 'How many bees are back at the hive?' 'Which is next?' 'How many more bees have to come home?' 'Are they all back home?'
- Increase the number of bees.
- Discuss bees with the children, what they look like, the noise they make, what they do, let the children taste some honey.

Mathematical development
This is a good way of introducing ordinal numbers (first, second, third and so on) without the children having to depend on knowledge. Consider it an ordinal number awareness-raising activity. Most children are quickly familiar with first, second and third, but even older children struggle to name and use ordinal terms higher than those.

ACTIVITY 8
The postman

Purpose
Counting a given set, one-to-one correspondence.

Vocabulary
Numbers zero to ten.

Resources
A door, painted on a large cardboard box, with an opening cut out for a letter box, various-sized addressed envelopes.

Activity

Based around the following rhyme:

My house has a big red door
The postman knows it is number four
It has a letterbox long and wide
The postman drops some letters inside.

One child acts as the postman and carries a sack containing about ten letters.

The children say the rhyme. The postman decides how many letters (zero to ten) he is going to deliver. These are dropped, singly, through the letterbox so that they can be counted as they drop through the door.

A second child acts as the householder and collects the letters from inside the box. These are then re-counted to see if the number matches the number delivered by the postman.

After this scene has been played a number of times, a variation could be played where the postman does not deliver the letters singly but delivers them in a bundle (having first counted them). Only the postman knows how many there are. The children then say to the postman:

> Through the letterbox long and wide
> How many letters did you drop inside?

The postman answers: 'I dropped *** letters inside'. The householder then comes from the other side of the door and counts the letters.

Extension

- This rhyme can be part of a class theme. Discuss the job of a postman. Maybe arrange for a postman to visit the school to talk with the children. Send a postcard to someone in the school (the caretaker, the headteacher). Why do we use stamps? Make a display of used stamps. Make a collection of different sizes, colours and types of envelopes. (These can be used for sorting.)

Mathematical development

Children need to match the counting rhyme to the actions. The posting action slows the counting rhyme right down, so that the numbers become separate. This will help children with their one-to-one correspondence. (Be careful that children do not count seven as two numbers because it has two syllables se-ven.)

Various-sized envelopes provide an opportunity to practise counting a mixed group.

ACTIVITY 9
A pair of legs

Purpose
Recognizing a pair as a set of two, without counting.

Vocabulary
Pair, one to two, twos.

Resources
None.

Activity

Based around the following rhyme:

A pair of legs to run, jump, skip and hop
A pair of lips to suck a cold lollipop.

A pair of ears to hear my friends talking
A pair of knees to bend so I can go walking.

A pair of arms to stretch up to cupboards high
A pair of hands to wave up to the sky.

A pair of eyes to see the flowers and trees
A pair of feet to kick through the autumn leaves.

All these things to do and see
I am so lucky to be me.

Ask the children to finish the sentence, 'I can see a pair of . . .' Make a collection of pictures of pairs of socks, shoes and so on. See the section in this book titled 'Pairs'.

Discuss with the children things that are called pairs but are only one thing, such as a pair of trousers, a pair of glasses, a pair of scissors, and why they are called 'a pair'.

Use a child to demonstrate, 'Alice has a "pair of feet". How many feet has she got? Yes, she has got two feet. Have you got a pair of feet? Show me.' Select another child, 'Joe has a pair of knees'. Repeat using a different child to demonstrate the pairs mentioned in the rhyme above and ask all the children to point to them on their own body. If there is sufficient space, the children could do the actions.

Read 'The pairs' rhyme to the children. Ask them how many legs, feet, eyes and hands, there are in a pair.

Say the rhyme again and ask the children to point to the pair of . . . at the beginning of each line. On the last word the children point to the centre of their chest.

Extension
- Make prints of pairs of hands and feet in paint.

Mathematical development
Often in maths we use words that are different but are asking children to take the same action or do the same calculation. 'Pair' and 'twos' is a good example of this. To ensure the children are not thrown by unfamiliar words it is good to 'parallel' the use of words. Another example is 'oblong' and 'rectangle', which are used similarly in early years maths.

ACTIVITY 10
We like numbers

Purpose
Recognizing a numeral (1 to 10). Knowing that numbers are used for a variety of purposes. Hearing large numbers spoken and seeing them in number symbol form.

Vocabulary
Numbers one to ten.

Resources
A set of home-made books to stick pictures in containing about ten blank pages and a sheet of brightly coloured paper for a wall display.

Activity

Based around the following rhyme:

My friend John
He likes number one.
Do you like number one? I do.

My friend Sue
She likes number two.
Do you like number two? I do.

My friend Rosa Lee – She likes number three. Do you like number three? I do.
My friend Ivor – He likes number four. Do you like number four? I do.
My friend Clive – He likes number five. Do you like number five? I do.
My friend Alex – He likes number six. Do you like number six? I do.
My friend Megan – She likes number seven. Do you like number seven? I do.
My friend Kate – She likes number eight. Do you like number eight? I do.
My friend Caroline – She likes number nine. Do you like number nine? I do.
My friend Helen – She likes number ten. Do you like number ten? I do.

The number book

Make number books for 1, 2, 3, 4 and 5; for example, *Our Book of Three*, where each page contains a set of three things, each member of the set being similar but not identical. These sets can be cut from drawings made by the children or pictures cut out of magazines or catalogues. Examples could be: three ice creams; three watches; three chairs; or three dogs. Put an appropriate caption on each page such as: Three umbrellas.

The number frieze

Give each child a large sticky label. Ask them which their favourite number is. This is written (in numerals) on the sticky label and stuck, in a random fashion, on the frieze paper. (It may be necessary to write the number for the children, especially as they may be large numbers.)

As each child adds his/her favourite number then he/she explains to the class what the sticker says and why it shows his/her favourite number. Reasons will vary and may include: 427 – the number of the house he/she lives in; five – his/her age; 101 (Dalmatians) – his/her favourite film; a million – because it is a big number and who doesn't want 'To be a Millionaire'?

Extension
• Make up similar rhymes.

Mathematical development
Using maths in context supports using and applying maths. Children have to 'pick out' the maths from the context. Later these skills are drawn upon in problem solving. Number names are known as the cardinal aspect of numbers.

Dice

Normally, dice are used in games to generate a random number. On the market there are dice with higher numbers than six but, to begin with, one to six dice are good because these are numbers that children will be increasingly confident with. There are several types of six-face dice displaying dots, numerals, colours and sometimes pictures. The random generation of numbers allows activities to have a 'game-like' feel to an activity, which can be motivating for the children. It also means that each child has the same chance as the next if a competitive game is being played. Large dice are ideal for short whole-class floor activities.

A stack of number cards can be used instead of dice. Playing cards with the court cards removed make a useful number pack. These have the added advantage of each displaying the numeral and the quantity. However, the use of playing cards may be a sensitive issue with some religious groups.

Dice with dots on are an excellent starting point, as the children can count the dots and match the last number in the count ('last in set' names the set) to the quantity displayed. As children become used to the dice patterns they should be able to recognize the pattern and name the quantity. When children reach this point it is important to discourage the counting and have confidence in the pattern.

To begin with children need to know that they read the top face of a dice. If a child is sitting down then the side of the dice will be in his/her line of vision. If he/she is standing, looking down, then he/she is more likely to read the top face. This can be an issue with large dice.

Dice with numerals bring their own challenges. When the dice has landed, the numeral may not be facing the child so he/she is required to recognize the numeral in any orientation. It is easy to muddle two and five as they are almost mirror images (reflections).

There will be a time when you would like the children to recognize the number and then apply the quantity to another situation, such as a board game. For children working with small quantities or where collections of objects are being generated, it might be useful to limit the numbers further, so that final totals are not too large. In this situation a dice with only ones and twos on it might be appropriate.

Please note that the singular for dice is die, but the word dice is used throughout as it is in common usage.

ACTIVITY 11
If it's a 3 clap your hands

Purpose
To recognize numerals and their associated quantity.

Vocabulary
Numbers one to six plus action words.

Resource
One large 1 to 6 dice

Activity

This is a game.

Roll the dice. The children have to count the dots and then respond with the right action. These can be introduced gradually. The children should be encouraged to name the number after the action. You should ask, 'How many dots are there?'

Actions that could be used include:

- If it's a 1, jump up and sit down, 'It's a 1'.
- If it's a 2, say 'Oooh, it's a 2'.
- If it's a 3, clap your hands (three times), 'It's a 3'.
- If it's a 4, touch the floor, 'It's a 4'.
- If it's a 5, raise your arms, 'It's a 5'.
- If it's a 6, say 'It's a 6'.

Extension
- Ask the class to make up some new responses to the above actions.
- Use a number dice (easier).
- Play it in PE with large movements.
- Play it in pairs with sounds only.
- Take up a bigger challenge and use a 9-sided dice.
- Play it using a pack of 1–6 cards

Mathematical development
The combination of counting/symbol recognition, action and saying the number allows the children to establish the names of the numbers, either related to the symbol or the quantity. The multi-sensory approach will help some children. The rhyme may help the children to remember, as it becomes a mnemonic. Games are a delightful way to reinforce and remember important facts. Children like to return again and again to some games. In this case they get to practise their maths as well.

38

ACTIVITY 12
Dots on top

Purpose
Counting with a one-to-one match of spoken numbers to objects, recognizing numerals and naming the last in a set.

Vocabulary
Numbers one to six.

Resources
One large 1 to 6 dice, 1 to 6 number cards.

Activity

One child rolls a large dice so that everyone can see.

'How many dots can you see on the top?'

The child then counts the dots (on the top face) and tells the class how many dots there are.

All count together as you point to each dot.

'Which card shows number 4?'

The children point to the number card which represents the quantity.

Another child takes a turn.

Extension
- Use a set of cards with dots up to 10 (for example, playing cards).

Mathematical development
One-to-one matching is sometimes referred to as one-to-one correspondence. The children need to match the counting rhyme with the same number of objects. Often children say the rhyme quickly and point slowly, ending with a random number. Sometimes they count objects twice or miss one out. They need to learn to be systematic. Pointing as they say the number helps. Children experiencing difficulty may need to have objects to count that they can physically move or place in a single line. 'Last in set' is the final number counted and tells you how many there are (cardinal number).

ACTIVITY 13
More or less

Purpose
To add or subtract
1 or 2.

Vocabulary
Numbers one to seven, more,
fewer (less), add, take away,
backwards, forwards.

Resources
One large dice, number
line (optional) and cubes
(optional).

Activity

One child rolls a large dice so that everyone can see.

'How many dots can you see on the top?'

The child then counts the dots (on the top face) and tells the class how many dots there are.

'How many dots would there be if there was one more?'

The child answers.

All count together as you point to each dot.

'And one more makes . . .?' Get them to join in the sentence.

Another child takes a turn.

Extension
- When the children are ready, ask for 2 more, 1 less and 2 less.

Mathematical development
More and less are easier in a single group context, as opposed to asking who has more (such as two bags of sweets, or two sets of cubes). This is the beginning of addition. The children can often manage to add on as they use the counting rhyme in the order they first learned it. Less is more challenging, as they have to count backwards or re-count leaving one off. One less is easier as they often remember what they have just counted, rather like an echo. This is something they need to practise.

Technically, when talking about quantity you should refer to 'fewer' and use the word 'less' when talking about measurement, however, 'less' is a term which children may be more familiar with. Forward and back might be vocabulary used with the number line.

ACTIVITY 14
Match the objects

Purpose
To count and then count again matching different objects.

Vocabulary
Numbers one to six.

Resources
One large dice and a collection of ten objects. These can be the same or, later on, a mixture of different types of objects.

Activity

Roll the dice.

'Count the dots on the top.'

Child counts the dots and correctly identifies how many.

'Come and choose the same number of dinosaurs.' (Objects can be used such as cubes, toy cars, teddy bears or a mixture of objects.)

The whole class counts together, with you or a child pointing at each one in turn.

Extension
• Use the mixed set of objects, or two dice added together for larger numbers.

Mathematical development
This activity is asking the children to transfer their knowledge to a new context: counting the dots, naming the quantity and transferring that knowledge to finding that quantity in a new set. The children often find sets of objects the same (for example cubes) easier to count than a set of mixed objects. It is important for them to count a set of mixed objects so that they realize that the counting rhyme can be used in a 'mixed object' context, and the names and order remain steadfast.

ACTIVITY 15
Adders

Purpose
To practise adding two numbers (number bonds/facts).

Vocabulary
Add, make, numbers one to 12.

Resources
Two dice (dots and then numbers) or number cards.

Activity

A child rolls two dice to show two numbers (for example 4 and 3). The class then have to add the dots.

The class give the answer (7).

'Do 4 and 3 always add up to 7?'

Encourage the children to give an opinion and then check by counting.

'What is 5 plus 2?'

Children answer.

Then show 5 and 2 on the dice and all count together.

Continue with other numbers generated by the two dice.

Extension
- Use dice with numerals.
- Use dice with higher numbers.
- Use three dice.

Mathematical development
Children need to be encouraged to move away from counting every time, to have confidence in known facts. This can be done by reversing the sequence. Ask for the answer and then go back and check. There needs to be a conversation about numbers being predictable. The answer to 4 + 3 is always 7. This is the beginning of learning number facts/bonds.

ACTIVITY 16
Count on

Purpose
To practise 'counting on'.

Vocabulary
Numbers one to 12.

Resources
Two large dice or dice cards (or a dice generator on the whiteboard).

Activity

'Roll the dice'

A child rolls the dice.

'How many dots are on the top?'

Child answers, '3'.

'Everyone, how many?'

The class repeat the child's answer (when correct).

'Roll the second dice. How many dots are on this (the second) dice?'

Class answer.

'Let's count on together; 2 . . .' (first number)

All count together.

'How can we check?'

(Count all the dots on both dice.)

'Were we right?'

Class: 'Yes.'

2 min
2 min

2 min
2 min

2 min

2 min

2 min

Extension

- Use number dice instead of dots.
- Use one dice with numbers to nine.

Mathematical development

Initially, the children learn to count all the objects using the number rhyme. If you are adding a number, you don't need to start at the beginning and 'count all'. Children need to learn to 'count on' from the first known amount. For example, if you knew there were 15 sweets in a bag and you are given another five, you would add 15 and 5. If you didn't know that 15 and 5 made 20 you would count on from 15 . . . 16, 17, 18, 19, 20. You would not tip the sweets out and count them all over again. 'Counting on' is a first step to adding.

ACTIVITY 17
The hidden face

Purpose
A guessing game leading to finding the difference and number bonds to 7.

Vocabulary
Numbers one to seven, opposite, underneath, on top.

Resource
One large 1 to 6 dice.

Activity

The dice is rolled.

'If 4 is on top, what number is underneath?'

(This begins as a guessing game.)

'Is there a pattern here?' 'Who thinks they know the number underneath?' (Give plenty of time, maybe several visits to the guessing game, for children to work out that the opposite sides add up to 7).

When the pattern is shared, continue the game, expecting them now to work out the answer, either by counting on or subtracting.

'If opposite faces add up to 7 and the top face is 3, what is on the face underneath?'

Extension

- Look at difference in other situations.

Mathematical development

This starts as a mystery, rather like a magic trick. It may be days before some children realize the pattern. Try to stop them telling the others for a while, so they get a chance to think. Maybe put the numbers on the board. Once they have seen the pattern, continue the activity but expect them to find the difference. They may do this by using their fingers and count on or subtract. It will help to discuss how to do this at an appropriate stage. Finding the difference is an important element of maths. The link between addition and subtraction is strong in this situation and either strategy can be used. The 'hidden' number is also good as they have to solve the mystery which later occurs in 'box arithmetic' and 'algebra'.

ACTIVITY 18
Money, money, money

Purpose
To select coins to represent quantity.

Vocabulary
Pence, numbers one to 20, recognition that a 2p piece is worth 2.

Resources
Dice, 1p and 2p coins, one dish.

Activity

A child rolls the dice. They then have to select the coins represented by the amount on the dice and place them in a dish.

Each child has a turn and then the coins in the dish are laid out in a line.

'How much is there altogether?'

All count together.

Start again.

Extension

- To make it easier use only 1p coins.

Mathematical development

When children count cubes or other objects there is a one-to-one relationship. In other words, each object represents one of the counting numbers. When dealing with money this relationship changes. A single 2p coin represents a quantity of 2 and a 5p coin represents a quantity of 5. Children are so used to practising a one-to-one relationship that they often find it hard to move on to representation. The visual cue of a single object/coin is telling them it is 1 but the number on the coin is telling them it is 2. They have to have 'faith' in the numeral or learn that a 2p coin is worth 2. A transition strategy that is useful is to tap the 2p coin twice when counting, as this gives the children a strong physical and aural cue.

ACTIVITY 19
More money

Purpose
To practise
'counting on'.

Vocabulary
Pence, numbers one to 11, recognition
that a 2p piece is worth 2 and 5p piece
is worth 5.

Resources
Large dice, large
representations of coins.

Activity

Start with a 5p piece. A child rolls the dice. He/she then has to select the coins represented by the amount on the dice and lay it beside the 5p piece.

'How much is there altogether?'

Child responds.

Check as a whole class.

There may be another question if the child chooses 1p coins: 'Are there other coins we could choose to make the number on the dice (2p and 5p)?'

Extension
• Change the
  starting
  amount.

Mathematical development
There is a close relationship between money and number. By using the dice to generate an amount, this can be translated into coins. The children's introduction to number is to count in 1s so there is a tendency to select 1p coins. This is an opportunity to move children on to selecting 2p and 5p coins. This builds towards selecting the least number of coins, which is later useful when giving change. By starting at 5p there is an opportunity to practise 'counting on'.

ACTIVITY 20
Two snake race

Purpose
To practise counting in a competitive game situation.

Vocabulary
Counting from one to 17.

Resources
Two snakes with 17 spaces for cubes, a dice with only 1s and 2s on it, 40 cubes or counters.

Activity

Two teams are formed and turns are taken to roll a 1s and 2s dice. The child who rolls the dice selects that number of cubes and places them on his/her team's snake. The first snake to have all the spaces filled is the winner.

As the game progresses and children are rolling the dice, you ask the others questions such as, 'How many cubes are there now?' and 'How many cubes do you need?' and 'Will you get there on this throw?'

Extension
- Make the game easier or harder, by varying the length of the snakes.
- Introduce a three on the cube or other numbers.
- Play board games such as Snakes and Ladders or Ludo.

Mathematical development
Introducing competition always increases the excitement. Taking turns is something to be learned too. This game is accessible to young children as it only requires counting to 2 on their own. Placing the cubes on the snake is an easy task. The game can be revisited, as it is competitive but does not require skill, only luck. It can then be visited at a higher level by making the snake longer and using a dice with higher numbers. Pairs of children may be able to play this on their own after it has been visited as a group activity. Taking turns is probably the greatest challenge.

ACTIVITY 21
Mystery number

Purpose
To establish number bonds and use missing numbers. 'Counting on' and 'commutativity'.

Vocabulary
Make, add, more, numbers from one to ten.

Resources
Dice, large number cards (small box and cubes for the extension activity) and a whiteboard to write on.

Activity

Hold up a card with a big number 7 on it.

'This is the number we want to make today.'

A child rolls a dice.

'How many more do we need to make 7?'

Children could count on using fingers, cubes or number lines.

One child answers.

All children check together with you.

Extension

- Use higher numbers.
- Write the calculation on the board (for example, 6 + ? = 10).
- Turn the calculation around and have a mystery start. For example, I have a number in the box and then roll the dice (3) and you say, 'it makes 7' (? + 3 = 7). What is in the box? (Using cubes in a box is visually helpful.)
- Use real or toy money.

Mathematical development

This is the beginning of algebra. You are asking children to find the missing number (which may, much later, be called X or be shown as an empty box). Commutativity is present when you can change the numbers in the calculation around and still get the same answer. Addition and multiplication are commutative. A much harder situation is to start with a missing or mystery number, as children do not then know where to start counting. This is where an understanding of the commutative law is important. Absence of understanding leads to guessing, or trial and error.

ACTIVITY 22
Jump to it

Purpose
To name a quantity and transfer it to action.

Vocabulary
Numbers one to six.

Resources
One large 1 to 6 dice.

Activity

One child rolls a large dice.

The child then has to jump the number of times shown on the dice.

Alternatively, the child could call out the number on the dice and the rest of the class have to jump that number of times.

Extension
• Choose different actions.
• Use number cards and extend the action to ten.

Mathematical development
Children need to be able to associate the name of the number with the quantity and realize that numbers represent the same amount whether it is objects or actions. Sometimes this is referred to as 'the three-ness of three'. This activity links dots (quantity) to the name of the set (number) to quantity (the jumps).

Use this space to record your own activity notes.

Floor activities

These activities involve the children in physically moving, so a large floor space is needed. You may be lucky enough to have a large classroom or you may be able to use the hall or playground.

Some of these floor games require a track. There are five main types of track. In order of difficulty they are:

1 Four straight tracks in a cross pattern meeting at the centre.
2 Straight parallel tracks (two or more).
3 A single blank track, straight or curved.
4 A stepping-stone track.
5 A single numbered track.

Having a track with numbers in the spaces can be very confusing for young children. For example, if a child is trying to play Snakes and Ladders and he/she lands on 4, he/she then rolls the dice and a 3 is seen. The child looks at the numbers on the track and may move back to the 3. Most of these floor activities use tracks with no numbers. If there are numbers then they are numbers connected with the dice. If a circular track is used a start/finish point should be indicated, otherwise the children continue to go round and round.

There are various ways the outline of the track can be drawn:

- lightly chalked on the floor (this will be impermanent and can be erased)
- painted in the playground (this can be more permanent and can be used by the children during playtimes)
- painted on material which is plastic coated (these are permanent but mobile and rolled up they will store in a relatively small space)
- painted on large pieces of cardboard (these are mobile but have a short life and will need storage space).

'People' floor games are an ideal opportunity for children to learn the rules and then a smaller table-top version of the board game can be made where counters replace children.

Playing games means that certain rules need to be established and skills need to be learned such as:

- How to take turns in a clockwise direction.
- When someone wins, others lose.
- How to move along a track.
- How to translate the number on the dice into moves.
- How to count the number of moves, not the number of spaces – a dice showing 3 means a child moves three times. Many children count the number of spaces including the one they are on. This process is known as 'counting on' and is later used in number line work.

Establishing rules is important. Consider whether a child needs the exact number to win or will a larger number be accepted? The larger amount is recommended to start with. After all, a larger number does get you to the end of the track. When a child wins, what of the other three children? Do they continue to play? Establishing these 'rules' will mean there are fewer disagreements when the children are playing and they have less teacher supervision.

ACTIVITY 23
The windmill track

Purpose
Reading a dice (dotty or numbers) and counting on (0 to 4).

Vocabulary
Numbers one to four, moves, counting on, jumps.

Resources
A dotty/number dice using the numbers 1, 2 and 3 (for example, 1, 1, 2, 2, 2, 3) and a windmill board (floor or table-top size).

The windmill track
Draw a cross, as on a windmill, with the four arms meeting at a central point. Split the four arms into 10–12 sections to make a track (like a path made of rectangular slabs), these could also be lightly coloured. Do not number the track sections. Where the tracks meet, draw a circle.

Activity

Four children stand one at each end of the cross-track. Call them Blue, Green, Red and Yellow. Blue begins and you say: 'This is Blue's turn.'

The dice is rolled, the face is shown to the children, Blue is asked to read the number, for example 2.

'That means you make two moves/jumps.'

Blue then moves/jumps the corresponding number. (It is important that the child counts the moves.)

Always move clockwise around the group, until you get back to Blue. Again, Blue's dice is rolled. Once the child is standing on the track it is more likely that the child will count the square he/she is standing on. Always emphasize the need to count the moves, not the spaces.

Extension

- Let a child, who is not involved in the game, roll the dice and call out the number.
- Add a number 4 to the dice (1, 1, 2, 2, 3, 4).
- Add a 0 to the dice (0, 1, 2, 2, 3, 4).
- The central section can be used to link the game with a current classroom theme. By putting a picture or model of a tower in the centre, the game becomes 'A race to the tower'; similarly it could be 'A visit to the zoo'. A box of pirate treasure in the centre circle and children wearing pirate hats changes the focus and adds to the excitement.

Mathematical development

This is a fun opportunity to practise transferring dice numbers or dots into board-game action. It is important that children count the hops or the landing point. This will help them to keep track of how many are added. They will need this skill later when adding and subtracting using a number line.

ACTIVITY 24
The side-by-side track

Purpose
Reading a dice (dotty or number) and counting on (0 to 4).

Vocabulary
Numbers one to four, move, jump, count on.

Resources
A dotty/number dice using the numbers 1, 2 and 3 (for example, 1, 1, 2, 2, 2, 3) and two, three or four parallel side-by-side single tracks (floor or table-top size).

The side-by-side track
Draw identical straight tracks with the same number of sections (like a path made of ten to twelve rectangular slabs). Ensure that there is a common base line and finishing line. There can be two, three or four tracks side by side. Do not number the track sections. These are like the windmill tracks but are placed side by side. Be aware that this makes it easier for the children to make comparisons and see who is winning and losing.

Activity

Each child stands at the bottom end of a track, on the start line. Decide which track will always go first, second and so on. Choose an order and be consistent, for example, maybe you always begin with the track on the left or the one closest to the door.

Continue as with the windmill track.

Extension

- Let a child, who is not involved in the game, roll the dice and call out the number.
- Add a number 4 to the dice (1, 1, 2, 2, 3, 4).
- Add a 0 to the dice (0, 1, 2, 2, 3, 4).
- The tracks could be drawn to represent various situations such as ladders against a wall (a race to put out the fire), train tracks (a race to reach the station), swimming lanes, running lanes for horses and so on.

Mathematical development

When using tracks as a support to counting on, children need to be clear about the technique of picking up the counter and counting as the jump is made and the counter lands. Encourage touching each square and saying the numbers out loud. This strategy will be very important later when using the number line for calculations.

It is always fun to play a game and most children like to compete if they have a chance of winning. Games are an excellent way of children consolidating their maths.

ACTIVITY 25
The single track

Purpose
Reading a dice
(dotty or number)
and counting on
(1–3 or 0–4).

Vocabulary
Numbers zero to
four, move, jump,
count on.

Resources
A dotty/number dice using the numbers 1, 2
and 3 (for example, 1, 1, 2, 2, 2, 3). A single
track, either straight or curved – floor or
table-top size.

The single track
Draw one track like a garden path made of
10 to 12 rectangular slabs, the path can be
either straight or curved. Do not number
the track sections. As there is only one track
this means that all the players will be using
the same track, so there is likely to come
a point where at least two players, maybe
all four, will be sharing the same section.
This adds to the fun but may also cause
confusion, especially as to whose turn it
is to move.

Activity

Each of the children stands at the bottom end of the track, on the start line.
Decide the order of turns (using colours may act as an aide-mémoire).

Continue as with the windmill track.

Extension

- Let a child, who is not involved in the game, roll the dice and call out the number.
- Add a number 4 to the dice (1, 1, 2, 2, 3, 4).
- Add a 0 to the dice (0, 1, 2, 2, 3, 4).
- The track could be used with a theme. For example, the way to the library, with each child carrying a particular coloured book; the way through the wood to reach Goldilock's house, with each child carrying a teddy bear wearing a coloured ribbon; or the trail of the spaceship to reach the planet.

Mathematical development

Translating dots on the dice to an oral number and then translating the number to the correct number of moves will initially be a challenge. Visually, there is support through matching dots on the dice to moves on the board but this is quite laborious and the translations should be encouraged where possible. An overt discussion of these steps could help some children. Frequent use of the dice will help the children to spot the patterns and be confident about the numbers they represent. Board games with tracks reinforce the counting on required when using the number line.

ACTIVITY 26
The stepping stone track

Purpose
Reading a dice (dotty or number) and counting on (1–3 or 0–4).

Vocabulary
Numbers zero to four, counting on, move, jump.

Resources
A dotty/number dice using the numbers 1, 2 and 3 (for example, 1, 1, 2, 2, 2, 3). A single track, straight or curved – floor or table-top size.

The stepping stone track
Draw one track like stepping stones across a stream, with about 10 to 12 stones, the path can be either straight or curved. Do not number the stones. As there is only one track this means that all the players will be using the same track, so there is likely to come a point when at least two players, maybe all four, will be sharing the same stone. The stones need to be large enough to accommodate the number of children. If using a table-top size version, then counters or objects will share a space.

Activity

Each of the children stands at the bottom end of the stepping stone track, on the start line. Again, decisions need to be made as to the order of which person will go first, second and so on.

Continue as with the windmill track.

Extension
- Let a child, who is not involved in the game, roll the dice and call out the number.
- Add a number 4 to the dice (1, 1, 2, 2, 3, 4).
- Add a 0 to the dice (0, 1, 2, 2, 3, 4).
- Stepping stones could lead across the river; the track could be made of footprints of a dinosaur, a snowman or a giant; another alternative is that they could be lily-pads and each child pretends to be a frog leaping across the lake, or small beanbag frogs could be used.

Mathematical development
This activity is further reinforcement of counting on techniques. As the children can be the counters, the physical aspect is fun. You might choose to play this outside with a chalk track drawn on the play area. This also gives children an opportunity to consolidate their learning in an informal, play context later, without supervision.

ACTIVITY 27
Islands

Purpose
Listening to number instructions/reading a number symbol and using the numbers to count from one to three.

Vocabulary
Numbers one to four, stop, count, count yourself.

Resources
A set of ten chalk circles (islands) big enough for four children to stand in, and a set of number cards 1 to 4, or dice.

Activity

Draw about ten chalk circles on the floor, space them well apart. Tell the children to move around the room but do not go inside the circles. Change the mode of movement to add interest, for example run, skip, hop, bunny jump and so on.

Shout 'stop' or use a different signal such as a drum.

On the island there can only be ___ people (call out a number, for example 1, 2, 3, 4).

The children run to the islands, there have to be the exact number of children that you called out in a circle.

If you wish the game to be competitive, the children are 'out' if they are not on an island, or if there are too many/not enough people on an island.

Play until there is only one child left to be crowned king/queen of the islands.

Extension
- Add numbers 5 and 6 to the dice.
- Hold up a number card instead of calling out the number so that the children will have to read the number symbol.

Mathematical development
Children find it fun to do maths when they can move about. This activity supports counting of quantity, in this case 'bodies'. They will be challenged to count themselves. It will also be a social challenge too, particularly when a child is required to move to another circle. Leadership skills may emerge here! You need to allow the children plenty of time to begin with to play this game and, as they play it again, they will get quicker. This is a simple example of using and applying maths.

ACTIVITY 28
Four corners

Purpose
Recognizing oral numbers and matching to numerals (0–10).

Vocabulary
Numbers zero to ten, backwards, sideways, forward, run, skip, hop, jump.

Resources
A set of large number cards and a set of small number cards.

Activity

Place a large number card in each corner of the room, for example 5, 2, 7, 0 (a chalk mark can be drawn on the floor but this is not necessary). The children move around the room, change the mode of movement to add interest, for example backwards, sideways, forwards running, skipping, hopping, jumping and so on.

'Choose a number.'

The children decide which number, they want to stand near.

Ask one child in each group to read his/her number.

Using the small set of number cards, face down, and only the four numbers on display, you choose (or ask a child to choose) a card and call out the number.

If you wish to be competitive, those in that corner of the room are 'out' of the game.

Play until there is only one child left.

For the next game, change the numbers in the corners; the winning child can choose these.

Extension

- Use number words to label the corners of the room.
- Use shapes instead of numbers to aid shape naming and recognition.

Mathematical development

Bringing together the oral and the numerical representations of the number is a key step. The physical nature of this activity allows the teacher to observe those children who are not sure of their number names or the numerals. This also gives them an opportunity to practise this matching in a fun way.

ACTIVITY 29
Find your seat

Purpose
Matching numerals to number names, reading the numerals, using positional language.

Vocabulary
Numbers to ten, in front of, behind, next to, at the end, first, last.

Resources
Two sets of number cards 1 to 10.

Activity

Discuss with the children places where seats may be numbered and why they need to be numbered (at the cinema, a concert, on a train or on an aeroplane). This activity is about finding your place in an arrangement of numbered seats, it is based on using ten chairs. The area could be being used for a concert, for story time, to watch TV, or the play area could be set up as a train or an aeroplane.

Place the chairs in short rows. Fasten numbers on the back of the chairs so the numbers are in order.

Choose ten children to form a line and give each one a number (not in sequence). Each child in turn has to find his/her own seat.

Once the children are correctly seated this activity is a wonderful arena for using positional language . . . Ask, 'Who is in front, behind, next to you? Who is at the end, in the first seat, the last seat, on the front row, the back row, the middle row?'

Extension

- Give one or two children the task of acting as ushers, showing a child to his/her place.
- Put up a plan of the seating with the seat numbers on. Put the children's names on the plan to see if they can find their seat numbers.
- If there are more than ten chairs being used and it is not appropriate to use higher numbers, use colours, for example blue numbers 1 to 10, red numbers 1 to 10 and so on.
- This activity could be used when the children have their snack (in which case it will be slightly different as the chairs will probably be arranged around tables). It could be a 'Monday task' to arrange the seating for the coming week.

Mathematical development

Positional language is important in maths. Simple everyday language about space develops to more accurate descriptions such as left and right, forwards, backwards, coordinates, compass directions and bearings. Children will also start to use directions with electronic toys such as Beebops and Roamers. Another development from this early work will be ordinal numbers such as first, second, third and fourth.

ACTIVITY 30
Catching the train

Purpose
Reading number symbols and counting (1–5).

Vocabulary
Numbers one to five.

Resources
A large group activity. Some number cards (four each of cards 1, 2, 3, 4, 5), a matching set of cards with loops of string attached to hang around a child's neck and a green flag.

Activity

The children sit at the side of the room in groups of six to eight. These are the people waiting at 'the station' for the train. From each group one child is selected (either by you or by the children in the group). These children are to be 'the engine drivers' of the trains.

Give each 'engine driver' a number to hang round his/her neck, for example 4. This number tells the 'engine driver' how many passengers can be carried on the train.

The 'engine drivers' move round the room making suitable train noises.

When you blow the whistle*, each 'engine driver' returns to his/her station and stands in front of his/her group of people. The correct number of passengers gets behind the 'engine' (hands on the shoulder of the person in front).

Check each train to ensure it is carrying the correct number of passengers (in this case four).

Ask the 'engine driver', 'How many passengers have you got? Are there too many/not enough?'

If, or when, the numbers are correct then the station master's green flag is waved.

When all the trains are ready, the whistle is blown again but only the trains with the correct number of passengers are allowed to leave the station. The others remain seated.

Repeat using different engine drivers and different numbers of passengers.

*Please note that some schools only allow the use of whistles out-of-doors.

Extension
- Initially, use the same numbers for each train, this makes it is easier to compare trains.
- Use different numbers for some of the trains, then the language of comparison can be used: 'Which is the longest train, the shortest train? Do any have the same number of passengers? How many more passengers has this train than that train?'

Mathematical development
This activity is an opportunity for children to practise counting. When the engine driver is not part of the count it is easier for the children to check they have the right number of passengers. This is also a useful activity for assessment, as you can see which children are using their counting strategies in an applied situation. This will indicate how secure children are in using their number knowledge.

ACTIVITY 31
The noise-maker

Purpose
Reading numerals and counting to 5.

Vocabulary
Numbers zero to five, clap, stamp.

Resources
A set of number cards with 0, 1, 2, 3, 4 and 5.

Activity

Read the children the rhyme:

> Let everyone clap hands like me, (clap, clap)
> Let everyone clap hands like me, (clap, clap)
> Come on and join in with the game, (clap, clap)
> You'll find that it's always the same. (clap, clap)

'How many times did we clap?' 'How many times did we clap altogether?' Teach all the children other noise-making words and the actions such as clap, jump, hop, stamp, shout 'Hi' and tap your nose.

'Jump three times' and the children do the actions. 'Make one clap' and the children do the actions. 'Stamp twice' and the children do the actions. As the children do the actions you need to count quite slowly, or their actions can be done so swiftly that they merge into one.

Ask different children to demonstrate, for example 'Clare is going to hop four times, see if you can count them . . . one, two three four hops. Well done.'

The children sit down. Ask a child, for example Simon, to stand at the front.

'Simon is going to be the noise-maker. What noise are you going to choose for him to make?' Simon is then, secretly, shown one of the number cards, this card is then placed face-down. Simon does the action noises and the other children have to count, silently, the number of claps (which should tally with the number on the card).

A child is asked the number. The number card is turned over. If the child is correct then it is his/her turn to be the noise-maker.

Extension
• Add other noisy actions. Make sure that they are easy to count.

Mathematical development
This is an opportunity for children to convert the numeral into a quantity. It requires the child to keep track of the finishing number (last in set) and to count the actions. It is easy for children to get carried away with the actions and do too many, so accuracy is required. Other children can count too, so all are taking part.

ACTIVITY 32
Copy cats

Purpose
Counting 1 to 5.

Vocabulary
Numbers one to five and the meaning of the chosen action words.

Resources
None.

Activity

The children need to know some actions which can be easily counted, for example, three steps backwards, two claps, two steps sideways, three hops, and so on (see activity: The noise-maker).

The children sit facing you (you are also sitting down). You need to use the same position as the children, as this signals the start and end of each section of the activity.

'I want you to copy what I do.' Then stand. The children stand. You touch the floor, the children touch the floor. You turn around, clap, cough and so on, and the children copy. The final action is always to sit down.

'I want you to watch carefully.'

The children watch as you stand, do an action while counting each time, for example 'I am going to do some jumps – one jump, two jumps, three jumps', then you sit down. You ask the children 'How many jumps did I do?'

Then all the children stand and copy your actions. They sit when the actions are completed.

This is repeated a number of times for various actions.

You demonstrate a short sequence: two claps; three hops; one turn around. 'How many claps? How many hops? How many times did I turn around?'

One child is asked to repeat your sequence of actions.

All the children stand and copy the sequence of actions.

Repeat this a few times.

Tell the children that this time they will have to do the counting themselves but that they have to do it silently. You demonstrate a short sequence of actions but do not count.

One child is asked to repeat your sequence of actions.

All the children stand and copy the sequence of actions.

Repeat, varying the actions and using a sequence of three actions.

Extension
- Lengthen the number of actions in the sequence.
- Ask a child to be the leader.

Mathematical development
This is a good activity for developing concentration. It will show which children can count and name the number of a set of actions by using the last number in the count. The activity requires the children to concentrate, remember and reproduce the actions in a nice little sequence, using their counting skills.

Number lines (washing line)

These activities involve the children using a number line in the form of a washing line, where the numbers are on cards, which are pegged onto the line. Using a washing line means that a card 0 can be used; the numbers can be moved around easily; and it can be fastened at a height that the children can reach the numbers. You can stand behind the washing line so that the children have a clear view, especially if the activity involves a puppet being used. For safety reasons ensure that the line is above head height of the tallest child.

The order of the number symbols should be permanently on display in the classroom. The basis of correct counting relies on a person being able to say the number order consistently. This is sometimes referred to as the counting rhyme. In order to know the number order the rhyme should be said and read frequently and repeatedly. The strength of using a washing line approach is that it reinforces the number order and can help a child to match the number name to the number symbol (numeral). The numerals can be reordered and the children challenged to re-establish the correct order or identify 'missing' numbers. The number line does not support a match between quantity and number unless you make one with pictures or dots.

The basis of being able to count is the ability to say the correct number order consistently (one, two, three . . .). Also, the children need to know which number word matches which numeral (for example, two – 2, five – 5, nine – 9 and so on).

The knowledge of the numbers to ten will vary with each child. Your judgement is vital with regard to determining the needs of individuals and the needs of the whole class. The teacher needs to decide:

- whether to begin the number order with zero
- whether to use the washing line to 10 immediately
- whether to use the numbers to 5 and then gradually add other numbers
- the amount of practice that is needed at each stage, how many times an activity needs repeating and when to move on to a new idea.

It helps if the numbers are in a large size (approximately 10 cm by 15 cm), and if there is an indication of the 'right way up' (flagging which is the top of the card by cutting off the top corner of the card or by drawing a line under each number or by shaping the card).

If it is not appropriate or convenient to use a washing line, then use another means of displaying the cards in a line so that the children can see and reach the numbers and move them. This could be on the wall using sticky tape or spread out on the floor.

It is important that the children are secure in their knowledge of the number order before they are asked to apply number knowledge such as 'numbers before and after', 'counting in 2s'. Insecure order of the numbers leads children into guessing and a loss of confidence.

ACTIVITY 33
Pegging out

Purpose
Matching the number word to the number symbol, reading individual number symbols in a random order (use 0–5, then 0–10).

Vocabulary
Numbers zero to five and six to ten.

Resources
Washing line and pegs, number cards 0 to 10.

Activity

Peg out the cards in order and say each number.

Encourage the children to read out the number words as each card is pegged up then read out the full sequence of the numbers.

Point to cards randomly and ask the children to read the card that you are pointing at. Repeat this until each card has been read out.

Ask a child to come and point to the cards (in order 0 to 10), while the other children read out the numbers when they are pointed to and not before. This turns the activity into a game with the child determining the speed of the reading.

Point to cards randomly and ask the children to read the individual card. Repeat this, asking individual children to read each card.

Starting card – point to a certain card (for example 3) and ask a child to read the numbers in order, beginning with the card and stopping at the last card on the washing line – repeat several times with individual children.

Stopping point – point to a certain card (for example 3) and ask a child to read the numbers in order beginning at zero and stopping at that card.

Extension

- Extend the washing line to include the numbers 6, 7, 8, 9, 10 for children who are consistent and secure in the number words and number symbols to 5.
- Peg out the first number, 0. Arrange the other number cards, in mixed order, in the children's sight but away from the washing line. Ask the children what comes next, after zero. Ask a child to find the correct card and peg it up. This extends the activity as children are not only saying the missing number but have to recognize the numeral.

Mathematical development

It is important that children can attach a name to each of the numerals. Initially, children learn the counting rhyme in order and find it very hard to start in the middle of the rhyme or put a name to individual numerals without starting at one. This activity promotes recognition of the numerals in any order. It is also good practice to encourage the children to start counting at different numbers. This will help later, when counting on when a second set is presented. It is also important to know when to stop counting. It is so easy to complete the counting rhyme when it is not needed and miss the end number. Knowing when to stop will be used when counting a set of objects. As you are working with a number line, this is an easy place to introduce zero.

ACTIVITY 34
Before and after

Purpose
The number order 0 to 10 and positional language; before, after, next to, first and last.

Vocabulary
Numbers zero to ten, before, after.

Resources
Washing line and pegs, number cards 0 to 10.

Activity

Peg out a number card (for example 4). Arrange the other number cards in mixed order in the children's sight but away from the washing line. Ask the children what comes after 4? One of the children finds the correct card and pegs it up. All the children read the numbers that are pegged up.

Repeat this using the words 'comes after' and 'what comes before' until each of the numbers to 10 is in place.

Allow the children thinking time by:

- Giving all of the children a set time before any answers are offered. When sufficient thinking time has been given, give a signal – for example, raise your hand – to show the end of the thinking time. Individual children can then be asked the answer or all of the children asked to raise their hands if they think they know the answer.
- The children sit with a partner and the first child whispers the answer to the second child, who raises a hand to show the answer has been given (with the next question the roles of whisperer and listener are exchanged).
- The children have a set of number cards and are asked to hold up the number card which shows the answer. Alternately, the answer could be written down. For practical purposes these last two probably require the children to be sat at a table.

Extension

- Look at the completed number line and ask the children if all the numbers are there. Encourage them to check by using questions such as: What do we say before/after the number 4? Which is the first number on the washing line? Which is next to the first number? Which is the last number on the washing line?

Mathematical development

Ordering the numbers is an important step in learning the numbers to ten. It is about matching the learned rhyme to the numerals. As the activity is repeated the children will be expected to know the sequence without starting at one each time.

Allowing the children 'thinking time' is important for many activities. Thinking time allows the children time to work the answer out for themselves. Children who are confident may well want to give the answer quickly. As a result, the children who need more thinking time or those who have not worked out the answer 'give-up' unless you control the answer giving.

ACTIVITY 35
Here's Hoppy

Purpose
Reading individual numerals in a random order (0 to 10). Correcting when the numerals are not in sequence

Vocabulary
Numbers zero to ten.

Resources
Washing line and pegs, number cards 0 to 10, a puppet (for example, Hoppy the Frog).

Activity

Introduce the puppet: 'I've brought a friend to help me today. Here is Hoppy the Frog. He has put out the cards ready for us.'

Tell Hoppy that the children are very clever at reading the numbers. Ask Hoppy to point to any number and then ask the children to read it out. Ensure that Hoppy waits for the children to read the number before pointing to another. The numbers should be chosen randomly, and not in sequential order. Gradually increase the speed until the numbers are being pointed to quite rapidly. End this part of the activity quickly, with Hoppy stopping pointing suddenly as if exhausted. Put the 'tired' puppet away for a rest and remove the numbers from the washing line.

Explain that while Hoppy is having a rest, we're going to learn something new and surprise him. Peg out the number cards on the washing line but place one card in the wrong order: for example, 0, 1, 2, 3, 4, 8, 5, 6, 7, 9, 10. Read the numbers in order with the children while pointing at them until the 8 is reached. Discuss with the children what needs to be done to correct this. Take down the 8. Re-read the sequence from 0 until the 9 is read after the 7. Discuss with the children what needs to be done. Replace the 8 after the 7. Re-read the sequence from 0 until 10. Ask the children if this is correct.

Take the cards down and say to the children 'Let's see if Hoppy is awake and then he can see what we have learned.' Peg the cards out with two in the incorrect order. Hoppy looks at the number line and shakes his head in disbelief. Say to the children 'Let's see if there is something wrong.' Repeat the task of correcting the order, with Hoppy's help.

Repeat by putting different pairs of cards out of sequence.

Extension
- Put more than two numbers out of order.

Mathematical development
Using a hand puppet is a useful strategy. You can interact with the puppet, showing surprise and disbelief. While many children would not know how to react if you, as the teacher, make a deliberate mistake, when the puppet gives a wrong answer the children feel less inhibited to correct the mistake. For example, the puppet could regularly place a number symbol upside down and the children respond by making a turning sign with their hand. It is important that the children know the numbers, are secure in their ordering and can start anywhere in the sequence.

ACTIVITY 36
Missing numbers

Purpose
Reading the number order in sequence (0 to 10).
Reading individual numerals.
Finding missing numbers from the number sequence.

Vocabulary
Numbers zero to ten.

Resources
Washing line and pegs, number cards 0 to 10, a puppet (for example, Hoppy the Frog).

Activity

Peg out the number cards on the washing line with some cards facing the children. The other cards will appear blank as they are pegged with their backs showing (for example 0, 1, –, –, 4, –, –, –, 8, –, 10). The children read out the number words of the cards they can see.

Point to the first card and ask one child, 'What number is written on the back of the first blank card?' Do the other children agree? How do they know? The child turns the card over to check. The card is placed face-forwards. Continue, in order, until all the cards are showing. Repeat this activity using different missing cards.

Using the puppet, 'Let's show Hoppy what we have learned.' Hoppy looks in amazement at the blank cards. He then points, randomly, to one of the blank cards. Ask a child to tell Hoppy what the number is. Hoppy checks by looking at the back of the card and makes a gesture to show 'yes' or 'no'. If 'no' then the number order is said beginning at zero until the card is reached and this should give a clue as to the missing number. Continue until all the cards are facing the children. This activity needs to be repeated until the children are confident at being able to say the missing numbers.

Extension

- Peg out some numbers with spaces between for the missing numbers. Arrange the other number cards, in mixed order, in the children's sight but away from the washing line. Ask the children what comes after zero. Ask a child to find the correct card and peg it up. This extends the activity as children are not only saying the missing number but also have to recognize the numeral.

Mathematical development

You are developing the children's ability to be consistent and secure in the number words and numerals 0 to 10, and recognizing the numeral without starting at 1 or 0. This is a good way to introduce zero as part of the number line. This is its ordinal property. Its other property, cardinal, is expressing lack of quantity, which is best expressed as an empty set or nothing left.

In order to gain maximum concentration from the children it is often better to teach a new activity and then use the puppet when practising.

ACTIVITY 37
Hop on and back

Purpose
Jumping/counting on and back in 2s up to ten.

Vocabulary
Numbers zero to ten, jumping on, jumping back.

Resources
Washing line and pegs, number cards 0 to 10, a puppet (for example, Hoppy the Frog).

Activity

Peg out the number cards 1 to 10. The puppet 'stands' on 3.

'Hoppy is going to do some jumping. Hoppy is going to make two jumps.' Hoppy shakes his head and looks down as if afraid of heights. Suggest to the children that they encourage Hoppy by counting the jumps. The puppet then jumps on two as the children say 'one, two'. Now he is on number 5 (in order to prevent the children from counting the initial card it is important that each of the jumps is counted and not the cards and that the final number is emphasized as the answer).

Repeat the 'jumping on two' using a different starting number. After a few illustrations ask the children to predict the landing number before the puppet demonstrates the answer.

Move the puppet until it 'stands' on number 7. 'Hoppy is going to jump back two'.

Hoppy shakes his head. Get the children to encourage Hoppy. The puppet jumps backwards with the children counting the jumps. Now he is on number 5. (It is important that the puppet is seen to be jumping backwards. This will help the children to differentiate the direction on the washing line between 'on' and 'back'.)

Repeat jumping on two and jumping back two using various starting points. After a few illustrations, ask the children to predict the landing number before the puppet demonstrates the answer.

Extension

- Jumping on and back different amounts, for example 'If Hoppy "stands" on 4 and jumps on three what number will he be on?' Demonstrate using the puppet. 'If Hoppy "stands" on 5 and jumps back one what number will he be on?' Demonstrate using the puppet.
- Using repeated counting on where Hoppy 'stands' on 4 and jumps on two (children predict the answer, 6), then jumps on two more (children predict the answer, 8), then jumps on two more (children predict the answer, 10).
- Use repeated 'counting back' in twos.

Mathematical development

It is important for children to be able to use the number line in both directions: counting on and counting back. It is good to encourage the children to predict the answers. 'What do you think it might be?' 'Why do you think that?' are two good questions that promote prediction.

ACTIVITY 38
Pegging pairs

Purpose
Recognizing a pair as two, without the need to count. Counting in 2s to ten.

Vocabulary
Even numbers to ten, pairs.

Resources
A home-made book to stick pictures in – containing about ten blank pages. Pairs of shoes, socks, gloves: things that are easily paired, for example the pair match in colour, pattern, size, type, decoration. The washing line and pegs.

Activity

Use pairs of socks, maximum five pairs. Give out the ten socks, one sock per child. One child stands up and holds the sock for everyone to see. The child with the other matching sock stands up. Peg the pair of socks close together on the washing line. Questions to ask: 'Why do these two go together? Why do these not make a pair? How many in a pair? Is this a pair of socks? Let's count.'

Repeat until all the pairs are on the washing line, peg the pairs together but leave a gap between the pairs. Count the socks individually. Count the socks and emphasize the even numbers 1–2 socks, 3–4 socks, 5–6 socks, 7–8 socks, 9–10 socks. Then ask the children to do the same.

Take the socks off the line, in pairs, fold them together and count two socks, four socks, six socks, eight socks and ten socks.

Hold up a folded pair. Ask the children 'How many socks are in this pair?' Unfold them to check. Ask the children to get a pair, two pairs, three pairs and so on. Each time ask how many socks there are and unfold the socks to check.

Count the folded pairs of socks (without unfolding them) – two socks, four socks, six socks, eight socks and ten socks.

Repeat the above activity using gloves. Shoes could also be used, placed side by side as a pair. They would need to be fastened in pairs or put into shoeboxes.

Extension

- Make a *Book of Pairs*. Use pictures drawn by the children or cut out pictures from magazines or catalogues.
- On each page of the book put a set of two which are normally considered to come as a pair, for example, wellingtons, slippers, shoes, trainers, hands, feet, socks, gloves, mittens, curtains, legs, eyes, arms, knees and so on. Put an appropriate caption on each page such as 'a pair of socks'.
- The children can make shoe prints using paint, each pair in a different colour. These can be cut out and pasted in a book or used as a wall display.

Mathematical development

Counting in twos supports development of even numbers. Later it can support answers to the two times table.

Finger counting

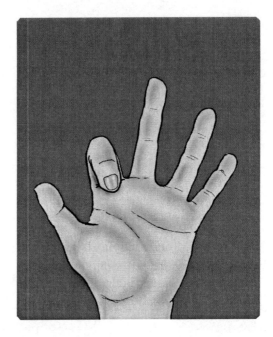

Fingers are a resource that children always have available. The use of the finger activities can help to reinforce an amount with a spoken number word; the matching of an amount to the numeral; conservation of an amount; and the skill of repeating a non-standard unit in measurement.

When using fingers to count, it is useful to have other resources used alongside to reinforce the connections between quantity, oral counting and numerals. A set of large number cards is a great asset. For a fun approach, finger puppets can be used.

You may choose to include the number zero, as a closed fist can represent the absence of quantity. You may also choose to build up to five and then later to ten. Many children find the tucking up of fingers quite difficult and use their second hand to help them. You need to ensure that, when illustrating the use of fingers, the children can see the back of your hands.

If they see the palm then the bent fingers can be seen and this can confuse some children. Similarly, encourage the children to look at the back of their hands and to fold the digits away for themselves. Initially, be prepared for it to take children quite some time to count and possibly 'hold down' the digits that are not needed.

Many of the finger activities in this section include the number zero. It is left to your discretion as to whether or when to include zero and the numbers 6, 7, 8, 9, numbers greater than 10 and counting in 5s.

You must also judge whether to use the word 'finger' and whether this includes the thumb, or to make a conscious decision to use the more accurate word digit, which is less familiar and may be confusing for children.

ACTIVITY 39
Fish fingers

Purpose
Using number names, matching an amount, using digits in differing orders.

Vocabulary
Numbers zero to ten, none, nothing.

Resources
Fingers.

Activity

This activity is used with the following nursery rhyme:

> One, two, three, four, five
> Once I caught a fish alive.
> Six, seven, eight, nine, ten,
> Then I let it go again.

Demonstrate by holding up your hand clenched like a fist with no digits showing. The back of the hand is facing the children. As the rhyme is spoken the fingers are revealed – one digit, two, three, four, five. For the line 'Once I caught a fish alive' the five fingers are used to make a swimming movement.

Continue until all ten fingers are showing. For the line 'Then I let it go again', all ten fingers are opened wide and then brought together and the hands are clapped.

The children repeat the above without you leading.

When the children have reached the point where this is easy, an extension could be: tell the children to watch carefully while the above is repeated but a different finger order is used, although the total is correct.

'What am I doing differently?'

The children repeat the rhyme actions, the number of fingers shown is correct but the children choose their own finger order.

Ask some children to show their number order and point out the differences but that the numbers are the same.

The children work in pairs, one says the rhyme, the other shows the finger numbers.

Extension
- Use the nursery rhyme 'One, two, buckle my shoe', which is slightly different in that it uses two numbers together.
- The children could also explore creating numbers on two hands which do not use all of the first hand. Doubles are a natural starting point such as two fingers on each hand being four

Mathematical development
By changing the order of the fingers children have to think about how many fingers are straightened. This moves them away from just repeating a pattern of opening the fingers in order and not thinking about how many.

ACTIVITY 40
Up-down fingers

Purpose
Orally counting from 0 to 5 and from 5 to 0 representing the numbers with fingers.

Vocabulary
Numbers zero to five.

Resources
Fingers.

Activity

Demonstrate that, by holding up a hand (showing the back of the hand) as a fist with no digits showing, says *zero*. Then show one digit and say 'one'. Continue with two, three, four and five.

The children repeat the above with you leading.

Hold up a hand showing five and say 'five', then show four, and say 'four', continuing down to zero. Ask, 'What did I do differently?'

The children repeat the above with you leading. Some children will be copying rather than counting, so, on a repeat, you no longer demonstrate. Ask the children to count up to five then count down to one using their fingers to show the numbers on their own.

Repeat this counting up, counting down a number of times until the children feel confident in saying both the number word order and using the appropriate number of fingers.

Extension

- Use a counting down nursery rhyme where the children are taking off/ counting down from five and from ten. These include:
- 'There were ten in a bed'
- 'Five fat sausages sizzling in a pan'
- 'Five currant buns in a baker's shop'
- 'Five speckled frogs'.
- When children are confident with counting up and down with the numbers zero to five, then consider extending using the above activity with the numbers six to ten.

Mathematical development

Counting down is an important skill, which will later support children's subtraction methods. Children also enjoy counting down to zero. Counting down involves learning the counting rhyme backwards. All the same things apply as when learning to count forwards such as the order and starting anywhere. Later this will be used for subtraction, but knowing how many you have taken away is really hard as you have to know the significance of where you start, say the numbers and at the same time keep track of how many you have subtracted.

ACTIVITY 41
Bunch of fives

Purpose
Matching oral numbers to quantity using fingers (zero, one to five and to ten).

Vocabulary
Numbers zero to five and ten.

Resources
Fingers.

Activity

Begin with the children illustrating the use of their fingers and counting up from zero to five.

'Now I'm going to mix up the numbers so you will have to watch and listen carefully. Watch and say them with me.'

Randomly show and says numbers zero to five. The children say the number word to correspond with the number of fingers. Remember to begin slowly, as many children will need to count every time. Judge when to speed up.

'Well done. Have you noticed that zero, one and five are the easiest?'

Illustrate these.

Then say the number words 'five, zero, one' and ask the children to show the finger amounts. Encourage them to do this without counting.

Repeat this using only zero, one and five in random order, have some fun and go faster as the children gain in confidence.

'How many is this?' Show the children ten fingers. 'Another easy finger number is ten. We can say the finger number without counting.'

Repeat the showing of finger numbers as above for zero, one, five and ten in random order, beginning slowly and then speeding up.

Repeat using all the numbers: zero, one, two, three, four, five and ten. Expect zero, one, five and ten to be done quite quickly but allow more time for two, three and four.

Extension

- Use rhymes with numbers but expect the children to respond quickly to the finger numbers for zero, one, five and ten.

Mathematical development

This activity is about responding quickly to the oral prompt. The numbers should be so familiar that the children no longer have to count from zero. Sometimes, early on, children believe that the answer will be different each time they count. You are looking not only for correct responses but also confidence.

It is good to introduce zero in this context, as the fist shows nothing or the 'empty set'.

ACTIVITY 42
Finger prints

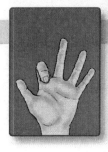

Purpose
Counting in 5s and 10s.

Vocabulary
Five, ten, none, counting zero to ten.

Resources
Paints, white card, about 20 cm square (two pieces per child).

Activity

Let the children practise making prints of their hands to form patterns. Keep reminding them, as they work, that each handprint has five fingers.

On one square of white card let each child make one handprint. On the second square of white card let each child make two handprints. The child can use any colour and orientation, and use only one hand or both.

Use some of these handprint cards in the following class activity. (Check the handprints are not blurred, it may be necessary to draw around the hands and fingers so that the fingers can clearly be seen and counted.)

'Show me five fingers.' 'Show me zero fingers.' 'Show me ten fingers.'

Repeat these a number of times, randomly using the numbers zero, five and ten.

Hold up one of the single handprint cards, 'How many finger does this show?'

As this activity is moving from object to pictorial counting, some children may need reassurance that there is the same number of fingers. Count the fingers to check.

Hold up different single handprints and ask the children how many fingers there are. If necessary, count to reassure the children that each handprint shows the same number of fingers even though they may be a different colour, size and orientation.

Repeat using the paired handprints.

Mix up the set of single and pairs of handprint cards and add a few blank cards to represent zero. Hold up the cards, as the children get more confident in saying the matching one, five, ten numbers, then speed up the exercise.

The task can be varied if you say the number aloud and individual children are asked to find and hold up a five card, a ten card or a zero card.

Extension

- Use bright colours to make the handprints (with fingers splayed) and cut them out, when finished with the counting. Use the prints to make pictures of birds where the handprints are used to represent body and tail feathers.
- Use some of these handprints in a wall display with 5 and 10 written on the card.

Mathematical development

This is another activity that gives children an opportunity to recognize the quantity of five without counting. Fingers are probably the most familiar context that children will experience for indicating five and ten. Give them more reassurance, time and practice so they can verify the answers and gain confidence. Confidence comes from the knowledge that five in any arrangement will 'always' be five.

ACTIVITY 43
Five finger exercise

Purpose
Counting in 5s to 30 (and upwards).

Vocabulary
Five, ten, 15, 20, 25 and 30, zero, none, counting zero to 30.

Resources
Fingers.

Activity

Begin with the children using their fingers to illustrate five and ten without counting.

Stand two children in front of the class, with their hands behind their backs.

Show and say, 'Zero, we can see no fingers.'

Initially, to avoid confusion, it is important that the children observing see the order is from left to right (as with reading). Begin with the first child on the left. The child holds up his/her right hand with fingers spread and you say, 'five fingers'. The child then holds up his/her left hand as you say, 'ten fingers'.

'Now we are going to have to be careful and think hard.'

The child on the right holds up his/her right hand and shows five fingers.

'How many fingers are there now?'

Help the children to count on from ten. Emphasize the answer: 15. The child holds up his/her left hand with fingers spread.

'How many fingers are there now?'

Help the children to count on from 15. Emphasize that the answer is 20.

'Let's do that again.'

Repeat the exercise, emphasizing zero, five fingers, ten fingers, 15 fingers, 20 fingers. Let the children count the individual fingers of the second child until they are confident of the answers 15 and 20.

Demonstrate again, using two other children. It is important that the children observe the pattern. Continue until the children can confidently say zero, five, ten, fifteen, twenty.

Extension
- For those children who are confident that the answer is 15 and 20, you can consider extending the activity to using three children and counting in 5s from zero to 30, up to five children and counting to 50.
- Let the children make handprints on card using three hands, four hands and so on, for the numbers 15, 20, 25, 30, and use them for display.

Mathematical development
It is important that children begin to accept that certain patterns are always the same, in this case five, ten, 15 and 20. This means that they do not have to count from the beginning but in many situations they will be able to 'count on'.

ACTIVITY 44
Fist towers

Purpose
Introducing the skill of repeating non-standard units in measurement.

Vocabulary
Fists, numbers one to eight.

Resources
Hands, plastic/wooden rods approximately 5, 10, 15, 20, 25, 30, 35, 40 cm long. These can be made up of a collection of everyday objects such as pencils, straws and so on.

Activity

Hold up one hand and makes it into a fist. The fist is placed on the table (little finger at the base, thumb tucked in). Ask the children to make a fist (check the little finger is at the base and the thumb is tucked in).

'I am going to make a fist with the other hand.' Demonstrate and then say to the children, 'Now I want you to make me two fists. Look, I can make a tower with my fists.' (Stand one fist on the table place the other on the top.) 'Look, I have made a two-fist tower.'

Let the children make a two-fist tower. Then ask each child in turn to show everyone how to make a two-fist tower.

Choose two children and ask them if they can, 'make me a three-fist tower? Now a four-fist tower?' Let the children practise this in pairs.

Depending on the dexterity of the children, continue to make a five-fist tower and a six-fist tower.

Let the children practise towers of one fist up to six fists.

Take one of the 5 cm rods, placing it vertically on the table. One of the children is asked to hold the rod.

'I'm going to see how tall this rod is.' A fist is made around the rod. 'See, it is one-fist tall.' Repeat using a 10 cm rod. 'This rod is two-fists tall.'

Using a 15 cm rod, ask a child to see how tall it is. A second child will be needed to make the third fist.

Let the children measure the rods using their fists.

Extension
- The above measuring activity uses many fists, repeatedly, as a non-standard, arbitrary unit. It is possible to demonstrate how to measure longer rods by repeatedly laying fists next to each other.

Mathematical development
It is good to use two objects to measure something which is longer than one object because the child can lay them next to each other. Measuring anything brings challenges with it in terms of the skill of using the measuring instrument. Things to look out for are matching the end of the measurer to the beginning of the thing to be measured, and not leaving gaps between the two measurers.

Dominoes

Dominoes is a traditional game which has been played in England for hundreds of years. More recently, sets of large dominoes have been available for use in schools. Not only can children play the game, which requires matching sets of dots, they can also be used for early counting and addition in mathematics. The highest possible number of dots in any section is six, on any domino it is 12, and combinations can generate higher numbers as required. Therefore it can be a useful resource. A large set can be used for a whole-class activity or a floor activity. Small sets can be used by pairs or individuals.

Numbers on dominoes are represented as dots, therefore this is a good source for counting. With two sets of dots there is the potential for 'counting all' or adding two numbers and therefore introducing simple addition. Each domino is a representation of the partitioning of two sets.

Simple addition begins with having two sets and combining them. Pushing them together and 'counting all' is the first step. Counting one set and then 'counting on' without re-counting the first set is a second step. The third is to apply number bond/facts and give a known answer. For example, knowing that two combined with five will always make seven. This requires memory and confidence about the 'always'. This comes through practising the number bonds in various situations and you directing the children's attention to the fact that the answer is always the same.

Children find games attractive and therefore motivating. This is a good way to practise and consolidate maths.

ACTIVITY 45
Who has . . .?

Purpose
Naming a quantity – last in set.

Vocabulary
Numbers one to six.

Resources
One set of large floor dominoes (card or real ones could be used).

Activity

Each child in the class has a domino.

Asks a series of questions, repeating the questions with different numbers. (Questions could be focused on one aspect each time the activity is used.)

'Who has (three) dots on one side (colour) of their domino?'

'How many dots have you got altogether?'

'Who has ten dots altogether?'

'Who has the same number of dots on each side?'

'Who has more than (five) dots altogether?'

'Who has less than (three) dots altogether?'

'Who has one more than (seven) dots?'

'Who has one less than (seven) dots?'

'Who has a (three) and a (four) on their domino?'

'Who else has two numbers which come next to each other?'

Extension

- Ask the children to work in pairs and make comparisons.
- Use the dominoes in 'count on' practice.

Mathematical development

There is a variety of vocabulary and mathematics addressed with the questions. Naming the quantity in the set by using the last number of the count is practice in applying the counting rhyme. Counting both sets of dots on the dominoes is an early form of addition, with the use of the vocabulary of 'How many altogether'. It is important to establish 'same' before introducing 'difference' when making comparisons. 'More than' and 'less than' are keywords in the development of the concept of comparison. Using very close differences of one and two are more easily managed, as they link closely to the counting rhyme which can then offer support. It may be useful that with this work a number line is easily visible. Introducing consecutive numbers reinforces number order and will be of use later.

ACTIVITY 46
Let's play dominoes

Purpose
Matching quantity sets.

Vocabulary
Dominoes, numbers one to six.

Resources
Large floor dominoes (normal sets for group work).

Activity

Play a class or group game of dominoes.

The dominoes are laid out at the front and you place one in the middle of the floor as a start. (Either use the full set (28) or a chosen selection.)

A child is either chosen or volunteers to find a domino that can be added to either end of the first domino.

The game continues in the same way until all the dominoes are used or none can be laid.

While the child is choosing, you can ask the rest of the class questions such as:

'What numbers will (Jamil) be looking for?'

'What number could you put on this end?'

'What numbers are we looking for now?'

Extension
- Play the game in a small group.
- Limit the number of dominoes to keep the game short.
- Play with picture or number dominoes. These can be created to fit with a topic theme, for example the seaside (seven pictures, 28 dominoes).
- Play shape dominoes using 'Logiblocks'.
- Play money dominoes.

Mathematical development
This is an early stage, matching the number of dots and checking that they are the same. With traditional dominoes the quantities are always set out in the same pattern, so children should learn to spot the pattern and have less need to count. This pattern spotting is an aid to realizing small quantities without counting. This will develop into other situations where the pattern is slightly distorted but still recognizable.

ACTIVITY 47
Line up

Purpose
Ordering totals.

Vocabulary
Order, numbers one to twelve.

Resources
Large floor dominoes.

Activity

Groups of three children are given five dominoes to put in order of their total number of dots. These can be laid in a row on the floor or on tables.

The children then need to say the numbers they have ordered.

The other groups can listen to check whether they are in order.

Extension
- Have more dominoes to order.
- For an easier activity, choose a consecutive number sequence.
- For a harder activity, choose a sequence with gaps, for example five, seven, eight, eleven.

Mathematical development
Ordering a selection of numbers is a reinforcement of the counting rhyme and its application to quantity. The sequence with gaps is more challenging, as children will want to find the 'missing' dominoes and this will challenge their use of the counting rhyme.

Use this space to record your own activity notes.

2D shape

There is a tendency to consider mathematics as learning about numbers. Mathematics involves a range of concepts involving rules and patterns and relationships. Much later on these develop into sophisticated areas of study such as chaos theory, calculus and algebraic equations. All these highly developed areas of mathematics have their routes in concepts that begin very simply and are accessible and even essential for young children.

Learning about shapes and their properties will lead into geometry and theories about shape and space and measures. The Ancient Greeks based most of their mathematics on theories of geometry.

The first stage of developing a concept about shape is to recognize and name different 2D and 3D shapes. The following activities focus on 2D shape although it can be argued that as 3D shapes are part of our environment, they should be introduced first. However, some of the names of 3D shape are difficult and 3D shapes have 'faces' with 2D names. It is up to you how you choose to approach this.

The second step is to identify the properties, which is the reason why this particular shape can be put in that category. For example, if the shape has three straight sides and is flat, it will be a triangle. Problems can arise if children are only shown equilateral triangles or triangles sitting on a horizontal base. If you do this, children will not recognize scalene triangles as triangles, or ones which are balanced on their tips as triangles. This is why using shapes which can be picked up and turned is good for concept building.

The drawback of using plastic shapes is that anything solid is actually a very thin 3D solid. You must choose when to introduce this fact. Initially the opportunity to handle shapes outweighs the fact that 2D only exists in drawings.

ACTIVITY 48
Find me

Purpose
Shape identification, leading to properties of 2D shapes.

Vocabulary
Triangle, square, circle, hexagon, rectangle, sides, corners, colours, numbers one to six.

Resources
Plastic shapes or Logiblocks or cut-out geometric shapes.

Activity

Lay all the shapes flat on the floor or table, with the children sitting around the edge.

'Who can find a triangle?' Get one child to select and hold it up.

'What shape has Jenny chosen?'

Class: 'A triangle.'

Continue with other shapes.

Then ask for a property, 'Who can find me a shape with straight sides?'

'What shape has Azziz chosen?'

Extension

- Add a new shape, for example, a pentagon, or get a child to choose a shape or property for the rest of the children to find.

Mathematical development

It is important for children to pick up shapes and move them around so that they can see them in different orientations. We tend to use the Logiblocks or plastic shapes for 2D work, when they are actually solids but this should not be a concern at this age unless a child raises the issue. It is important to get the children to observe, feel and identify the properties. Properties feature strongly in later maths on shape and in data handling.

ACTIVITY 49
Tell me something about . . .

Purpose
To use the properties of 2D shapes.

Vocabulary
Triangle, square, circle, hexagon, rectangle, sides, corners, colours, numbers to six.

Resources
Plastic shapes or Logiblocks or cut-out geometric shapes.

Activity

Lay all the shapes flat on the floor or table, with the children sitting around the edge.

'Find and pick up a triangle' (They can do this individually although it may be better, if you have enough shapes, to each pick up a triangle at the same time.)

Continue with another shape.

Get a child to ask the other children, 'Find and pick up a . . .'

After the children can identify the shapes correctly, move on to properties.

'Tell us something about your triangle.' For example, 'It has three points/corners.'

'Can anyone tell us something else?'

Extension
- Add a new shape, for example a pentagon.

Mathematical development

It is always good if the whole group is busy rather than watching one child engage with the teacher. All choosing a shape at the same time is a good strategy and then asking one child to give more information, then inviting others to contribute. This activity enables children to identify simple shapes, putting a name with the shape. For shapes to be recognized in many situations, the children need to be able to realize that they have particular properties. For example, a triangle has three straight sides and three corners. This knowledge will enable children to transfer the concept of a triangle to many different sized and shaped triangles. It is rather like seeing a spaniel as belonging to the set 'dog' and not realizing that dalmatians, alsatians and poodles are all dogs. This activity is a good assessment task.

ACTIVITY 50
It's different because . . .

Purpose
To compare 2D shapes by property.

Vocabulary
Same, different, triangle, square, circle, hexagon, rectangle, sides, corners, colours, numbers to six, bigger, smaller, curved, straight.

Resources
Plastic shapes or Logiblocks or cut-out geometric shapes.

Activity

Lay all the shapes flat on the floor or table, with the children sitting around the edge. You pick up two shapes, for example, two triangles.

'Is there anything the same about these shapes?'

Child: 'They both have three corners.'

'Tell me something that is different?'

Child: 'This one is bigger.' (Could be, curved, straight, one side, three sides, name of the shapes and so on.)

Extension
- Get the children to choose different shapes and comment on 'same' and 'different'.

Mathematical development
Looking at 'same' and 'different' is developing children's skill of comparison. Children find 'same' much easier to understand than 'different'. This is possibly because 'different' can have many answers, whereas 'same' is visually obvious. This activity builds on their understanding of the properties of shape and the language that accompanies it. Move from being the introducer of the language to expecting the children to construct sentences where they use the language. This is much more tangible when they have objects to describe and they are comfortable with the shape vocabulary which has previously been developed.

ACTIVITY 51
Shape snake

Purpose
To secure
properties of shape.

Vocabulary
Same, different, triangle, square, circle,
hexagon, rectangle, sides, corners,
colours.

Resources
Logiblocks, picture of a
snake's head (A4 size).

Activity

Lay all the Logiblock shapes flat on the floor or table, with the children sitting around the edge. Pick up two shapes with one common property, for example, thin, and lay them next to each other, which begins the snake's body.

'The first is a thin red triangle. Next to it I am going to put a thin blue rectangle. They are both thin. Who can find a shape to put next to the rectangle which has something the same about it?'

A child adds to the snake, saying what it is that is the same.

'Make the snake longer. The shape must have something the same as this one.' (Point to the last shape.)

The snake's body grows as long as possible, either in finding properties or in the time allowed.

Extension

- For an easy extension, the children can play this on their own either as a snake or as in dominoes, when you can add to both ends.
- A harder extension is to require two properties rather than one or remove the colour option.

Mathematical development

This is a game situation which children find enjoyable. No one is eliminated and it is alright to help each other, therefore there is lots of participation. The mathematics is the recognition of property in shapes. In this situation the children have to find a particular property to continue the snake, therefore they are required to apply their knowledge. The snake game also restricts what can be put down, so the children have to match their choice with some property to the previous shape. This comparison is easy with one common property required, but if you use the harder extension it becomes much more challenging. There is a tendency for children to select colour, so there may come a time when you say they cannot choose colour so that they focus on other properties.

Boxes, bottles and bags

Apart from all these resources beginning with B, they can also be used to help the children develop their mathematical thinking. This thinking will take them across a range of activities promoting maths, including number, data handling, shape and measure.

By placing objects in a box it gives a group of objects an identity, known in maths as a set. By isolating them in a box from the world around them the objects take on the feature of a group that belongs together.

Boxes and bags can hide things too. One might consider this the very roots of algebra where there exists an 'unknown', in later years to be referred to as 'x' or 'y'. At this level, the unknown is a guessing game but, like detectives, the children can be introduced to reasoning about what a hidden object might be. Feats of memory and deduction become involved. Both are skills which will support reasoning, a much valued aspect of mathematicians.

Children find playing with water and sand exciting. Filling and pouring, floating and sinking are engaging parts of a child's world and are also the beginning of scientific understanding. Their contribution to maths is equally important. In the concept of measures it is important to begin to understand about capacity. Children will learn about how much something holds, whether the bottle is full or empty, or even half full. They will be able to count how many cupfuls are needed to fill the teapot and whether this bottle holds more or the same as that bottle. Comparison is a key element of measurement.

On a practical level, bottles should be plastic. There should be a set of similar as well as a collection of different containers available. Transparent bottles are better than opaque ones. Food colouring is a safe way of making the water show up.

ACTIVITY 52
Hiding

Purpose
Recognizing (and writing) numerals 0 to 9.

Vocabulary
Numbers zero to nine.

Resources
A large set of number cards (it is important to be able to distinguish the top edge of each card, cutting off one of the top corners is a useful strategy, not only is it visible but it is also tactile). A box or a cloth bag larger than the cards

Activity

Put the numeral cards in the bag/box and slowly pull one out until just over half can be seen.

'What number do you think this is?' . . . 'Who else thinks it is number 6?'

'Does anyone think it is another number?' 3. 'Who else thinks it is number 3?'
Ask the children to look at the numbers on display in the classroom to help them.

'Let's look carefully. Which way do we draw the top of a 6 and a 3?'

Ask the children to draw a 6 and a 3 in the air.

Pull out the card and show the children the hidden numeral.

Put this number back in the bag.

Repeat, showing different numerals. (Be aware that children may need to see over half of the numeral to know whether it is 8 or 9; 2 or 3.)

Extension
- Use a set of cards with domino spot patterns and the set of shape cards.

Mathematical development
Some children find it difficult to recognize numerals when they are presented a different way up, so this activity is good for securing recognition of the features of numerals. This is also an opportunity to point out where the numeral begins when writing it. Children can confuse 2 and 5 as they are almost mirror images. Six and 7 start with the same sound so they can be confused. Seeing only half the number can be a challenge as 5 and 7 might look similar, as may 2 and 3. Getting the children to observe closely and develop cues will help them read and write numerals correctly. Similar is not enough, it has to be exact.

ACTIVITY 53
Take five

Purpose
Conservation of five, partitioning of five, counting on.

Vocabulary
Numbers zero to five.

Resources
Five small toys and a small cardboard box with no lid.

Activity

Let the children become familiar with the toys, count and re-count them so the children are sure there are only five toys.

Turn the box upside down. Let the children see that all five toys are put on the table and are covered with the box.

'How many toys are hiding?'

Repeat this a few times and each time reassure the children that there are five toys by counting them.

Any child who does not realize that there are still five (conservation of five) is not ready to go on to the next part of the activity.

Count the toys – five – then, without the children seeing, hide four under the box and put the fifth one on the top of the box.

'How many toys are hiding?'

Children may not know how to find the answer, so using the fingers to illustrate is a useful strategy.

'There were five toys.' Count five fingers and hold up your hand to show the five fingers with the back of the hand facing the children.

'Now I can see only one toy.' Put down all but one finger. 'How many are hiding?' Turn your hand around so the children can see the hidden four fingers.

'There should be four toys hiding, let's see.' The box is turned over to reveal the four toys.

Hide a different number of toys, including none. Encourage those children who need help to use the hand strategy.

Extension
- Repeat using ten toys, as this can again be linked to ten fingers.

Mathematical development
Children need to realize that if there are five objects, even if they are moved around or hidden and nothing taken or added, there will still be five objects (conservation of quantity). Some children may use a visual approach and be able to 'see' the number of hidden toys. This is a useful method but it is usually limited, as it can only be applied to small numbers. When the children have played this activity many times and are confident, then the counting on method could be introduced.

ACTIVITY 54
Posting boxes

Purpose
Learning a new number or practising a 'problem' number (0–10).

Vocabulary
Numbers zero to ten, as appropriate to the focus.

Resources
Three posting boxes and a set of cards showing numerals or amounts.
The posting boxes and cards: make three posting boxes. (You could use plastic cylindrical containers about 20 cm tall.) Cut a posting slot in the lid. It will be necessary to label and re-label the posting boxes, so removable stickers or wipeable material could be used. Make a set of number cards so that they fit through the posting slot. The content of the cards depends upon what is being practised (see below).

Activity

A child is being introduced to a new number or needs to practise a particular number, for example 5. One posting box is labelled 5 the other is blank. Use a set of sorting cards containing a mixture of single-number symbols but with a high proportion of 5s. The child sorts the cards into the boxes, 5 for the 5s, the other box for all the number symbols 'not 5'. When the child has completed the task, in the child's presence, open the 5 box saying, 'All the cards in here should be number 5. Let's see.' And on opening the other posting box: 'All the cards in here should not be number 5.' Discuss any in the 'wrong box'. A pattern of errors may be seen, for example the child is confusing 2 and 5, as they are both in the 5 box.

Use the same boxes but give the child a different set of cards. These have dots on them to represent 0, 1, 2, 3, 4, 5, 6, with a high proportion having five dots. Repeat as above. A few errors may be as a result of miscounting but the activity may reveal a pattern of errors, for example the 5 posting box contains cards with 4 spots (the child counts saying 1, 2, 4, 5 but uses the 5 as a name not a dot, mis-applying the counting rhyme).

A child is confused with the number symbols 6 and 9, so one posting box is labelled 6, the second 9, the third is left blank for any other numbers not 6 or 9.

A child can count three spots but cannot match the counting to the number symbol '3'. Put a '3' on one posting box and leave the other one blank. The card set will have one, two, three, four spots, with most being three spots.

Extension
- The posting boxes can be used for matching number symbols to written number names, matching shapes and matching letters of the alphabet.

Mathematical development
This is an excellent assessment activity as it will show the children who make consistent errors. It can also be used as a consolidation or remedial exercise. Another advantage is that, if necessary, the contents of the jars can be examined later.

ACTIVITY 55
Green bottles

Purpose
Using non-standard units and ordinal numbers.

Vocabulary
First, last, in the middle, numbers zero to ten.

Resources
Eleven identical 2-litre plastic bottles, a plastic cup or small mug and some green food colouring, funnel, small labels with cup symbols on them.

Activity

Help the children to put a cupful of water into one of the bottles (a funnel is useful for this task). Add a little of the green food colouring and screw the top on, tightly.

Put two cupfuls in the second bottle, three in the third and repeat, until the tenth bottle has ten cupfuls in it. One bottle is left empty.

Ask the children to put the bottles in order. Ask questions such as 'Which bottle is first?' 'Which is last?' 'Which bottle is in the middle?' If the children have begun with the bottle containing the greatest amount of water, then ask if they could order, beginning with the empty bottle (or vice versa).

Make labels to hang around the neck of each bottle showing, pictorially, one cup, two cups and so on. Put the bottles in random order and ask the children to hang the labels around the correct bottles.

Use 0 to 10 numeral cards to order the bottles.

Extension

- These bottles make an attractive and useful display.
- Use the bottles with the rhyme 'Ten green bottles'.

Mathematical development

It is important at this stage that the bottles are identical, as variations in bottle shape make the task very difficult. If the bottles are identical the judgement is often made by height. Later, children will need to move on from height judgements. The labelling of cupfuls will aid this as it is a non-standard measure. (This is a measure that is consistently the same size but it is not a recognized one such as litres or millilitres.) The children who link the number of cupfuls to the amount of water are confirming their judgement with further evidence. This is a good beginning to their reasoning skills.

ACTIVITY 56
Number boxes

Purpose
Making a set by counting non-identical objects and combining two sets. Conservation of quantity (0–10).

Vocabulary
First, last, in the middle, numbers zero to ten.

Resources
Eleven identical plastic containers with tight lids and a box of about 80 mixed, small objects.

Activity

Put a label on the side of each container, numbered 0 to 10.

Give the children a container each and ask them to put the correct number of objects inside. Check, or ask another child to check, before the lid is fastened down.

'Put the containers in order. Ask questions such as 'Which is first?' 'Which is last?' 'Which is in the middle?'

If the children have begun with the container containing the greatest number of objects then ask if they could order the containers, beginning with the empty container (or vice versa).

Ask questions such as 'Find me a box with three inside, with seven inside, with one more than this box, with one fewer than this box.'

Take a container and place an object on top of it. 'If I were to put this inside the box it would have the wrong number on it. What label would I have to put on it?'

Take two boxes (for example, 2 and 3).

'If I put all the things in these two boxes together how many do you think there would be?' Tip out the contents and count them. Repeat with two more boxes (use only small numbers). Repeat with three boxes.

Extension

- Use this activity (all the boxes need not be used at once) with individual children who need counting practice.
- Use the activity on a daily basis with different individuals.
- Vary the task by giving the children the filled boxes and asking them to write the correct labels for the front of the boxes.

Mathematical development

When children first learn to count we tend to present them with similar types of objects such as cubes. If objects are different we often ask children to sort them into groups with similar properties and ask them to count the number in each group. However, number can be applied to anything, so it is good practice to count objects that look different. In this way, children learn that the number is an abstract concept which can be applied to any situation where you want to measure the quantity.

ACTIVITY 57
Shelling out

Purpose
Estimating and counting.

Vocabulary
Numbers to ten.

Resources
A collection of similar objects up to ten in number (shells, leaves, toys) in an open box or tray, no overlap, plus a cover (cloth or lid).

Activity

Put four shells in the box.

'How many shells do you think are here?'

Uncover the box for a few seconds. Go around the group getting an estimate/guess from each child.

'Let's count them.'

You and the children count together.

'Who made a good guess?'

'I am going to change the number of shells. See if you can guess how many there are now.'

Extension

- If the children are able, they could play this in pairs without an adult present.
- Use a few more shells.
- Use a mixture of objects (which may be harder).

Mathematical development

Estimation is a skill which starts with guessing but improves as children become familiar with situations. Each time they receive feedback ('Let's count the shells') they should be able to make a better estimate in the future. It is important to get the feedback in-between estimates.

Most adults make their estimates based on pattern spotting. For example, if five objects are arranged like the symbols on a pack of playing cards or dice then the guess is likely to be accurate. Slightly distorted but familiar patterns aid estimation of quantity. Quantities above ten are almost impossible to estimate unless they are organized into a recognizable pattern, such as pairs, or into sub-group patterns such as seen as two five patterns. Later on, with large numbers, it is more realistic to give estimates such as, 'Between 20 and 30'.

ACTIVITY 58
Look and tell

Purpose
To observe different properties of objects (leading to sorting).

Vocabulary
Various descriptive words – in sentences if possible.

Resources
A tray with a miscellaneous collection of objects on it (for example, pencil, scissors, box, stapler, apple, doll, car, Lego brick, leaf, stone, shell, bell, Biro, photo, plastic shape, plastic dinosaur, tape measure and so on).

Activity

Show the children the tray of objects and invite the children to tell you something about any of the objects. This can be asked of the whole group or by taking turns.

After an initial run through, impose the rule that no one can say the same thing. Each child must identify a different feature.

Select one of the objects and ask each child to tell you something about it. (This makes the children really look at the differences.)

Extension

- You could ask the children to identify something the same about two of the objects. This could be developed with more mathematical shapes.

Mathematical development

This is a very early form of data handling. Before children can sort data they have to be able to notice the properties of what they are sorting. This activity asks them to closely observe objects and select properties. The third task can be very challenging if sustained, requiring children to search for things to say that have not already been said, such as what it is made from.

They may need an initial prompt, but will enjoy returning to this activity with different objects. It is an excellent plenary activity. It is also an open-ended task where children are unlikely to be wrong.

ACTIVITY 59
Wet, wet, wet

Purpose
Comparison, ordering and exploring capacity, conservation of liquid.

Vocabulary
The same amount, more water, less water, empty, full, half full, least, most.

Resources
Three transparent plastic identical jars, three other shaped transparent plastic jars, paint or cake colouring (optional), water, bucket or water tray.

Activity

Pour the same amount of water into three identical jars. Discuss whether they all have the same amount, or if any jar has more, or if any jar has less?

Pour some water from one jar into another.

'Which jar has more now?' 'Which jar has less?' 'Have any jars got the same amount in them?'

'Can you put the jars in order with the jar that has the most at this end (points to one end)? Make sure that the jar with the least water in it is at this end (points to the other end).'

'Tell me something about the amount of water in these two jars.'

Then pour the same amount of water in each jar again and then pour all the water in one of the jars into a new, different-shaped jar.

'What do you think has happened to the amount of water? Is there more, less or the same?'

When the children have offered their opinion, pour the water back into its original jar where it should look the same as the other two. Ask again about the amount of water.

Let the children play with the jars and the water. Then ask them if they have found out anything about the water.

Extension
- Use more extreme shaped containers (tall and thin, wide and shallow).

Mathematical development
The comparison of the same amount when it takes on a different shape is one of the aspects of mathematics young children learn to recognize (conservation). Jean Piaget carried out a series of famous experiments which showed that most children go through three stages of conservation. Initially children make judgements from the visual appearance of the situation. Gradually logic takes over when they realize that if nothing has been added or taken away there must be the same amount, whatever the visual differences.

Cubes

Cubes are a delightful resource. Friedrich Froebel was one of the first educators to use wooden cubes for early mathematics. His mathematical resources can be seen on display at Roehampton University, London. Today, most classrooms have sets of plastic cubes. Unifix cubes have the added feature of fixing together into columns and multilink cubes can be used to make cuboids and other weird shapes. Most of the activities in this section use the cubes apart so that the children can count them easily.

Counting objects can be a challenge for some children. The ultimate is to look at a small quantity and recognize the pattern. Sophisticated counters can look at larger quantities and mentally divide them into sub-patterns, which they then add together. This, however, is a long way from young children's starting point in counting.

Problems with counting objects occur when children fail to match each number to one object. This arises from saying the counting rhyme as one long string of words and then pointing to the objects out of time with each word. The rhyme needs to be applied one word to each object. The children need to slow down the rhyme and point to the objects in turn. Practise this together, modelling the process for the children.

If the cubes are in a random group, children often count some of the cubes more than once. To help children count you might need to get them to place the cubes in a line so that they have a starting and finishing point. If they are still having difficulty, get them to lift up the cube as they count and place it somewhere else, in a box if necessary.

Cubes can be used as measuring instruments. These would be considered as non-standard measures, although the multilink cubes have edges of 2 cm. The cubes can be either lined up against an object or two 'measuring' sticks can be used hand-over-fist style.

Cubes are also excellent for data collection. They can be used first of all on a one-to-one representational basis. For example, 'All those who like strawberry lollies come and take a red cube. Those who like orange lollies come and take an orange cube . . . Now, let's put all the red cubes in a row . . .' Later cubes can be used to represent more than one object.

ACTIVITY 60
Build a tower

Purpose
Comparing height.

Vocabulary
Same, taller than (shorter than) (height).

Resources
Pairs of children need between 16 and 20 multilink or unifix cubes to share.

Activity

Ask each child to take a handful of cubes and build a tower. Then ask them to line up all of their towers.

'Who has towers the same height? Is your tower taller than Jay's?'

Undo the cubes, take another handful and repeat the process. Get children to respond with the statement, 'My tower is the same as . . .'s' or, 'My tower is taller than . . .'s'.

Introduce 'taller than' separately from 'shorter than' and when the children are secure bring both phrases together in one statement.

'Is your tower shorter than Jane's?'

'My tower is shorter than Jane's but my tower is taller than Jay's.' (This is much harder and children may not be ready for a double statement.)

Extension
- Use more cubes.
- Ordering in groups of threes; use words such as tallest, taller than, shorter than, shortest.

Mathematical development
The language of comparison has the same syntax across most measure situations. Where two objects are being compared the language of direct comparison is used. Introducing the phrase 'taller than' is easier for young children to understand than just the word taller as it indicates the comparison required.

Tallest and shortest are the superlatives and are used when ordering three or more objects. Then comparative language is used as well. For example, 'Mine is the tallest. It is taller than Jane's. Jane's tower is taller than Jay's. Jane's tower is shorter than mine. Jay's is the shortest. It is shorter than mine and Jane's.'

The difficulty is that one object can have two relationships which children find confusing. In the example above, Jane's tower is taller in one comparison and shorter in another. It is best to introduce the terms one at a time, hence 'taller than' to start with.

ACTIVITY 61
Number towers

Purpose
To match numerals to quantity.

Vocabulary
Numbers one to ten, make, how many, count.

Resources
Number cards from 1 to 10, multilink cubes or unifix cubes.

Activity

Lay the cards out and ask the children to build a tower on each card. The tower must have the same number of cubes as the number on the card.

When the towers have been built then you can ask some of the following questions:

'How many cubes are there in this tower?' (pointing)

'You choose a tower and tell me how many cubes are in it.'

'If I had a card with this number on it, how many cubes would I need to make the tower?'

Show the children a tower. 'Which card would I put with this tower?'

Extension
- Take the cards away from the towers and ask the children to put them back with the right tower.
- With the children not looking, remove one of the cubes and ask them which tower is now wrong.

Mathematical development
It is important for children to link quantity to saying the numbers and recognizing the numeral. This activity promotes these links.

ACTIVITY 62
Which is missing?

Purpose
Linking quantity to the numeral.

Vocabulary
Numbers to five.

Resources
Big number cards 1 to 5 and a pile of 25 cubes.

Activity

Place the numbers on the floor or table and then invite a child to place the right number of cubes on the card.

'What number is this?'

'Put that number of cubes on the card.' Everyone count the cubes while he/she does it.

Repeat with the children placing the cubes on the other cards.

'Now I want you to close your eyes because I am going to take one cube away and I want you to tell me which card has the missing cube. You may have to do some counting to work it out.'

Extension
• Use cards from one to ten.

Mathematical development
There are many things children need to know about early number. In this activity, recognizing the name of the numeral is the first step. The second step is to identify the quantity that it represents. Counting in order and establishing the last name as the number in the set is implicit in the actions of placing the right number of cubes on the cards.

ACTIVITY 62
Passengers on the bus

Purpose
Practical addition and subtraction in a real-life context.

Vocabulary
Everyday language which indicates addition and subtraction. In this story, getting on and getting off the bus, more, less.

Resources
Toy people or cubes. An outline of a bus drawn on A4 paper.

Activity

Tell the story. At the same time, each child models the story using the resources. At the points with the asterisks you should pause and help the children and check that they have the right number of cubes.

Mrs Clippie, the driver of a one-man bus, set off early in the morning to drive along her usual bus route. She had driven along this route so many times that she knew most of the people who caught her bus.

At the first stop Mrs Rag and Mr Brush were waiting. They both had cleaning jobs in the big office block in town. They climbed aboard and Mrs Clippie said, 'Good morning' as they paid their fares.*

At the next stop a stranger got on the bus. She looked in a hurry and as she paid she said she had a train to catch, the early train to the city for an important meeting.*

At the third stop Mr Sunday got on and showed Mrs Clippie his bus pass.* He was a teacher at the local primary school and he liked to be early so that he could get everything ready for the children. 'Good morning Mrs Clippie, how are you today?' 'I am fine thank you Mr Sunday', she replied.

At the next stop Mrs James got on.* She worked at the post office further along the route.

No one was waiting at the next stop so Mrs Clippie drove past it without stopping. Mrs James then rang the bell for the next stop and, as the bus came to a halt, Mrs James came down the gangway and thanked Mrs Clippie before getting off.* As soon as she left the bus, two children got on and showed Mrs Clippie their bus passes.* They were going to breakfast club at the big school, which was why they were so early.

The next stop was the station which was near the office block, so the woman in a hurry, Mrs Rag and Mr Brush all got off.*

At the next stop Mr Sunday said, 'Goodbye and thank you' and got off the bus.*

As the bus went on its way, how many passengers were still on it?

Extension
- Any other story such as those involving farmyard animals, cars and dinosaurs could be substituted for the bus journey.
- Sing 'Wheels on the bus'.

Mathematical development
This activity is a series of additions and subtractions placed in a context. It may be easier for some children to have a context. It probably depends on how familiar they are with the context. The ritual of travelling on a bus has its own language and procedures. This could be confusing for those who are not used to bus travel.

The handling of objects to represent the quantities involved makes the calculation easier as the quantities are visually and physically present and feats of memory are not required. If this was purely a mental activity it would be really challenging to keep track of what is happening. Interestingly, if the calculation is represented in numerals it would be a lengthy, multi-step calculation:

+2 +1 +1 +1 -1 +2 - 3 -1 . . . not to be recommended!

ACTIVITY 64
Cube collection

Purpose
Quantity recognition and counting (last in set names the set).

Vocabulary
Counting to ten or twenty.

Resources
Dice with 1s and 2s, 30 plus cubes in a central pile.

Activity

The children take it in turns to roll the dice and collect the number of cubes as shown on it.

After a set number of goes, each child counts his/her cubes. The child with the greatest number of cubes wins the game. (You need to judge how many rounds will generate a manageable total. Also, it is best to keep games short and start again so that motivation is maintained and there are several opportunities to win.)

Extension

- A dice with higher numbers can be used or more rounds played so that higher totals are generated.
- A dice with numerals could be used.
- Number cards instead of dice can be used and the correct number of cubes placed beside them. (This is a good assessment activity.)
- Small toys or plastic dinosaurs can add attraction to the collecting.

Mathematical development

The one-to-one match with the dots on the dice will help the cube collection. Links with numerals can be made by using a dice with numerals or a pack of number cards.

Using the dice makes this a random activity and therefore one that can be used with mixed ability groups, as they have an equal chance of winning. More able children, however, may need the extra challenge of the higher numbers or collecting money.

Collection games such as this can lead on later to place value with grouping in tens.

ACTIVITY 65
Give and take (board game)

Purpose
To match quantities and find totals.

Vocabulary
Take, give, total, altogether, numbers one to fifteen.

Resources
Large sheet (A2 size) with a circuit drawn on it, which is divided into lots of squares. In some of the squares write instructions such as 'take 1', 'take 2', 'give 2' and so on (use more 'takes' than 'gives').
One counter and one dice (1 to 2).
Pile of cubes (30+) in the centre.

Activity

The counter is placed on a blank square. The children take turns to throw the dice and move the counter. If it lands on a 'take' square, the child takes that number of cubes from the central pile. On the 'give' squares, cubes have to be returned to the centre unless the child has none.

After a set number of turns (possibly five each), children count up how many cubes they have. The winner is the child with the most cubes.

Extension

- Increase the number of turns.
- Increase the numbers on the circuit.
- Use 1p or 1p and 2p pieces.

Mathematical development

This game can be tailored to the knowledge level of the children by adjusting the quantities and the number of turns. Keeping the game short and playing again is often a useful strategy for gaining attention. You will need to judge what level is appropriate for the children you are working with.

Games are very motivating and often children wish to return and play them again. Sometimes it is possible to have a game that two or three children can play without adult support. Learning about taking turns, winning and losing are often issues with young children.

ACTIVITY 66
What's next?

Purpose
To develop the language of probability and to experience prediction based on evidence.

Vocabulary
Colours, sure, certain, might, likely, unlikely, impossible, what chance is there?

Resources
A small box, five cubes, each of a different colour (five objects could be used).

Activity

Show the children each of the cubes, naming the colours. Then place them in the box.

'What colour might I take out first?' (Encourage the children to make sentences such as, 'It could be red.' Or 'It might be red, blue or green.' Try to move them on from guessing to using their memory and reasoning skills.)

Take one of the cubes out. 'It is red. What colour might I take out next?'

The children again suggest colours. You could challenge some children with, 'Why do you think it will be green?' and 'What can't it be?'

Continue to remove the colours. The children will begin to realize that they can be sure about the result. For example 'It must be blue or yellow' and finally, 'It must be blue.'

'Are you sure?'

Child, 'Yes.'

Extension
- It might be easier to start with three cubes so that it is easier for the children to remember.
- A harder version would be to have two of the cubes the same colour.
- You could increase expectations of children by requiring them to respond in sentences.

Mathematical development
Many people believe probability should be introduced later in the junior school and that it mainly involves tossing coins and playing with packs of cards. The language of probability occurs in the everyday world and should be drawn into mathematics. For example, what chance is there of rain today? Probability is about examining the evidence and making a prediction based on that evidence. This is something we should encourage children to do, as it is a major part of reasoning skills which also contribute to successful problem solving.

ACTIVITY 67
Colour coding

Purpose
Sorting and counting (last in set is the quantity in the set).

Vocabulary
Colours, numbers one to ten.

Resources
About 30 cubes, other objects can be used such as sorting sets, plastic shapes or natural objects (for example, a mix of conkers, leaves, cones and shells).

Activity

Each child has a pile of cubes (about 15).

'Sort the cubes into little piles, each pile with cubes of the same colour.'

'Tell us the colour of each of your piles.'

'Count your red cubes. How many red cubes have you got?' (Repeat with other colours.)

If appropriate you could ask, 'How many do you have altogether?'

Extension
- A greater number of cubes could be used.
- Objects where a particular colour is the main feature but not the total colour may be used such as toy cars. (This requires the children to make a decision about dominant colouring and therefore which group to place the object in. They may choose to place it in-between two colour piles.)

Mathematical development
The children need lots of opportunities to apply the counting rhyme and name the last in the set. This activity lays the foundation for sorting, which is one aspect of early data handling.

As the cubes are sorted into piles, children may need some help in accurately counting a random group of objects. This can be achieved either by pointing, lining the cubes up and then counting, or moving objects one-by-one to a new position as they are counted.

ACTIVITY 68
Softly, softly

Purpose
To introduce counting in 2s.

Vocabulary
Numbers to ten.

Resources
Ten cubes for each child (multilink, unifix, Lego bricks or any other small, uniform objects).

Activity

Each child and you has ten cubes in front of them.

'Count your cubes up to ten.'

The children all count their cubes to ten (pointing or moving as they count).

You arrange your cubes in pairs, each pair below the previous pair.

'We are going to learn how to count in 2s.'

Demonstrate whispering one and saying two out loud, whispering three and saying four out loud and so on, up to ten.

The children then arrange their cubes in pairs and they 'whisper count' together. After which they practise on their own.

Then demonstrate the counting again but this time point and be silent when counting the odd numbers.

This is repeated with the children joining in, after which they practise on their own.

Finally they repeat it altogether.

Extension
- Can the children count the pairs without pointing or moving the cubes?
- Can children repeat the counting in 2s rhyme without the cubes?
- It is possible to return to this activity and use other groups for counting. (This should not happen too soon.)

Mathematical development
Lining up, pointing or moving objects when counting really supports children, as they can organize the data and keep a sense of place. This is a step further in creating a regular pattern and counting 'sub groups' of 2. Later this can be a strategy for counting larger quantities such as creating groups of 10s, which supports place value and is the basis of our number system. Money is often placed in groups worth £1.

The counting in 2s rhyme is very common and one that children learn early on. It is the beginning of odd and even number properties, and one of the number rhymes which match the answers to the times tables.

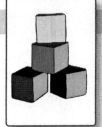

ACTIVITY 69
What's under the cloth?

Purpose
Simple addition and subtraction using memory.

Vocabulary
Add, take, numbers to six (or to ten).

Resources
A cloth (tea-towel size) or box, cubes or group of similar objects.

Activity

Show the children five cubes, count them together and then cover them with a cloth.

'How many cubes are under the cloth?'

The children reply.

'Let's see if you are right.'

You remove the cloth and they count them together.

Cover the cubes with the cloth again.

'I am going to take one away.' (Show the children the cube that has been removed.) 'How many are under the cloth now?'

The children give their answers and then the cloth is removed and everyone counts.

The activity is repeated, but this time you remove two cubes.

The activity is repeated with the removal of a different number of cubes.

The starting number of cubes can be varied.

A further stage is to take some cubes away and then return some under the cloth so that it becomes a two-step calculation.

More cubes can be introduced at the returning point so that the final number is greater than the starting number.

During the activity you should ask individuals how they worked out their answer. This will enable other children to gain a strategy for solving the problem.

Extension
- Use more cubes.
- Make the adding and taking sequence longer.
- Use different objects such as a leaf, a conker, a shell, a stone and a walnut.

Mathematical development
Using the cloth makes the objects unseen but tangible for most children. Children could use their fingers to keep track. Varying the objects emphasizes the calculations. Counting can be applied to mixed sets of objects, not just objects with similar properties.

Other resources

Things rarely fit into easily defined groups and it would be a shame to limit maths to the resources so far referred to, therefore this section has been created to contain some further activities using different resources which can be used to support maths. The collection is miscellaneous and, hopefully, can be added to. Please treat it as a stimulus for using anything you feel you can draw on to support mathematical thinking with your children, whether it be the Lego set for symmetry or the farm animals for mathematical storytelling.

A student, talking about her teaching practice, was very impressed with the Reception teacher she had been working with. Apparently, the teacher seized every opportunity to talk maths to her children throughout the day. And the children were really good at maths as a result.

In this section there are activities which promote the measurement of length, the ordering of objects by volume, counting on, number recognition, the ordering of numbers and the recognition of numbers.

Measurement covers many contexts including capacity, volume, mass (weight), length, time, angles and temperature. The earliest roots of all these are to develop language to describe such as tall, short, large, small, hot, cold, day and night. The next step is the ability to compare two objects or situations. Again this involves language: taller than, shorter than, larger than, smaller than, hotter than and so on. The third step is to order more than two objects. Here the language and thinking become tricky as both comparative and superlative language come into play and one object can have two properties. For example: Jamil is the tallest; Sara is the shortest; Amy is in the middle but we have no name for the one in-between. We can say Amy is taller than Sara, but we can also say Amy is shorter than Jamil. It starts to get confusing and children will need lots of visits to this maths. It is useful to introduce and practise terms one at a time and only combine them when the children are secure.

An electronic whiteboard activity has been included. There are many excellent programs available now on the whiteboard. There is software that can be programmed easily by the teacher to create maths appropriate for the children they are working with. Electronic whiteboards have really 'taken off' in English primary schools. There is the potential to use interactive whiteboards with younger children, particularly when they can touch the screen and make things happen. Making thing happen is why the Beebop and Roamer are so attractive to children, so we have included some activities to get children started on these too.

ACTIVITY 70
Long, longer, longest

Purpose
Comparison of length.

Vocabulary
Longer than, shorter than, longest, shortest, in order of length.

Resources
Three pencils of different lengths or strips of card or straws, and three pieces of string of different lengths.

Activity

Using, for example, three different length pencils: 'Can you put these in order of length? Put the longest at this end.'

Children order the three objects.

'Is this pencil the longest?' (Point to the middle pencil.)

Child responds.

'Which is the shortest pencil?'

Child points to the shortest.

'How do you know?'

Child . . . (for example, 'Because this one goes further').

Other questions you could ask include:

- 'Which pencil is longer than this one?'
- 'Which pencil is shorter than this one?'
- 'Find me a pencil longer than this one' (picks up the longest). Not possible.
- 'Tell me about these two' (encourage the children to use the correct language).

Extension
- Use the same language in different contexts. Use the three pieces of string curled up, as they are not immediately visually comparable and will require the children to straighten them before making a comparison. Children can also make shapes and glue them to card and talk about them to others. Choose objects where the difference is less, so the judgement needs to be made more accurately.

Mathematical development
Comparison of length is one of the easiest measures to make. However, it does require children to line up the starting point. Later this will connect to using a ruler. Having something like a stick as the starting point might help the children. Initially use objects which have a strong feature of length and a weak feature of width and so are visually obvious in their length difference. When understanding is secure, challenge the children with objects which are nearly the same length. The string, when curled, is visually challenging and children may judge the length by the visual appearance. Piaget describes this in his conservation experiments.

ACTIVITY 71
Stones

Purpose
Ordering objects by size (3D/volume).

Vocabulary
Larger than, smaller than, largest, smallest, in order of size.

Resources
Stones or other objects of different sizes (three per child). To begin make the objects obviously different in size.

Activity

Lay out a set of three stones out of order.

'I seem to be in a muddle, can you help me put them in order of their size? Where should I put this large one?' 'And the smallest?'

'Can you put your stones in order of size, largest at this end?'

When the children have sorted their stones;

'Which is the largest stone?'

And then, as appropriate, further questions:

- 'How do you know it is the largest?'
- 'Which is the smallest stone?'
- 'Is this stone smaller than this one?'
- 'Is this stone larger than this one?'
- 'Tell me something about the size of these two stones.'

Extension

- Use stones more closely matched in size (or use conkers, boxes, leaves).
- Order five stones.

Mathematical development

In this activity, comparisons are being made about three-dimensional properties. The concept is really about the space taken up by the object which is its volume. As the children's mathematics develops they will be able to measure more accurately. They might, much later, return to this concept through weighing or even later by displacement to prove they are right. It is quite hard to judge volume if the objects are of a similar size or very different shapes. Children use visual cues to make a judgement, which is understandable, as they do not yet have other ways of making comparisons. This task could lead into weighing but should not be rushed.

ACTIVITY 72
Toys go home

Purpose
Recognizing a number symbol (1–6).

Vocabulary
Numbers one to six.

Resources
A number symbol dice 1 to 6 and a toy floor track (see below for details).

Toy floor track
This consists of a single twisted garden track with 12 to 20 sections. Each section has a number but these are not consecutive. The numbers used are 1 to 6 and may be in the following order 2, 5, 3, 1, 6, 2, 4, 3, 4, 1, 6, 4, 5, 1, 4, 1, 6, 3, 5, 4. On the last square is the picture of a house door with a number on it. In this case it is house number 4.

Activity

Each child chooses a small toy. The toys are lined up at the beginning of the game (this is the order they will move and take their turn).

Tell the children that the toys are trying to get home (the door at the end of the road).

The first child rolls the dice, reads the number and moves his/her toy to the first/nearest square with that number on it.

The second child rolls the dice, reads the number and moves his/her toy to the first/nearest square with that number on it (this may be before, after or the same number square as the first child).

The third child rolls the dice, reads the number and moves his/her toy to the first/nearest square with that number on it.

The first child rolls the dice, reads the number and moves his/her toy to the next square with that number on it, always moving towards 'home'.

First toy home wins.

Extension
- Increase the numbers to nine and using a 1 to 9 dice.

Mathematical development
Unlike the 'child activities' where the child is the moving element, here the child uses a toy to represents him/herself in the game (as later a counter will represent his/her position on a board). When a child is part of the game he/she is often only aware of his/her own position, by using a toy the child has an overview of the game.

This is a good activity to practise reading the numbers on the track as they do not come in the usual order, so the children must be able to name the numerals as well as count the quantities on the dice.

ACTIVITY 73
Toys on the move

Purpose
Understanding and using language of position on a number line.

Vocabulary
Next to, before, after, between, one more, one less, same as, biggest, smallest (zero–ten).

Resources
A large number line, large number cards or carpet tiles with the number symbols 0 to 10 on them

Activity

First of all, ask the children to put out the number cards in a line, in the correct order beginning with 0.

Each child chooses a small toy. The children sit facing the number line, each holding a toy.

Refer to the toys, not the children. The doll is going on number 3 (the child holding the doll puts the toy on number 3). The car is on number 4, the teddy on number 7 and so on.

Instructions are given as to how the toys will move, such as: the doll is moving down 1; the car going on to the biggest number; the teddy is going on the number between 2 and 4.

Two toys may be on the same number, this does not matter.

The owner of the toy should be the one to move it.

You can vary the language according to the ability of each child.

There is no obvious end to the game but it is appropriate to finish with all the toys on the same number.

Extension

- Extend the language to include:
  2 more than; 2 less than; the next
  number bigger than; the next number
  smaller than . . .

Mathematical development

The children need to recognize the
language which allows movement along
a number line. This later leads into work
on addition and subtraction. The activity
also develops the children's ability to
follow instructions. The toys make it an
attractive activity. The activity can be
used for consolidation or assessment.

ACTIVITY 74
Beebop

Purpose
To give directional instructions (mathematical space).

Vocabulary
Forward, backward, left, right.

Resources
Beebop, Roamer or other electronic programmed toys, paper pathway, empty plastic bottles, empty cardboard box, as appropriate.

Activity

Children should have an opportunity to program the toy to move forward for a set distance. Developing from this, move forward and turn left or right, and move forward again. Simple goals can be created as a challenge. The following are some examples:

- A 'yellow brick road' made from paper taped to the floor. Either straight or with one turn to the left or right.
- A plastic bottle as a skittle to be knocked down or 'shunted'.
- Two skittles forming a goal.
- A cardboard box on its side as a 'home' to aim for.

Extension

- Pathways which require right-angle turns. Narrower pathways between large Lego brick walls.

Mathematical development

Children's development of their understanding of space is sometimes neglected and rarely attributed to mathematics. Yet later on they will develop the measurement of space through the study of area, compass points, coordinates, bearings and vectors. These early activities help develop children's language of space and their judgements about length and angle. Into this comes the ability to begin to estimate distance and angle when programming the toy.

ACTIVITY 75
Join the dots

Purpose
Forming the shapes of the numerals (writing).

Vocabulary
Numbers one to ten.

Resources
Electronic whiteboard notebook or A3 sheets of paper, pen.

Activity

Prepare a series of sheets/electronic pages, each with dots outlining one of the numerals from 1 to 10 in random order.

Ask the children what number the dots represent and then asks one child to join the dots of a numeral.

Emphasize the starting point and the direction.

Extension
- Increase the numbers.
- Use the number sewing cards, marble runs or sand trays to practise forming the numerals.

Mathematical development
Recording can be done with tally marks, but once children are familiar with the numerals it is time to get them to practise forming them in the right way. This shared activity gives you an opportunity to teach children where to start and which direction to go in when creating the written numeral. Some children find this a challenge, as many numerals begin at the top left and first letters often begin at the top right. Confusion can lead to number reversal.

ACTIVITY 76
Fishing for fives

Purpose
Recognizing numerals.

Vocabulary
Numbers one to five.

Resources
A hoop, several sets of 1 to 5 number cards, a dice.

Activity

At the simplest level, the cards are laid face-up in the hoop and you ask a child to find a card with a particular number on it.

A second level, is to roll a dotty dice and the child has to find the numeral that matches the number of dots.

At a third level, the cards could be turned over so it becomes a memory game.

At a fourth level, the children could do combinations of two number cards to match the number of dots, for example card 2 + card 3 = 5 on the dice. (A zero card is useful at this level.)

Extension
- Each of the above is progressively more difficult. Further challenge can be achieved by increasing the range of numbers.
- Sing the song, 'One, two, three, four, five, once I caught a fish alive'.
- Use two dice.

Mathematical development
Initially this is simply matching the oral version of the number to the numeral. If the higher level activities are used, they draw upon matching quantity to the numeral, then memory of position as well and the final activity requires knowledge of lower level number bonds.